This is the fourth edition of the original publisher's issue of *Managing Differences*. Other editions and printings are also published in Dutch, French, Japanese, Korean, Polish, Romanian, Russian, Spanish, and Swedish.

General inquiries and requests for information about foreign language editions may be sent to:

MTI Publications
5700 West 79th Street
Prairie Village, Kansas 66208-4604
USA

Website: **www.mediationworks.com**

E-mail: **mti@mediationworks.com**

What others say . . .

"Dr. Dana is an expert on the world's most important task – the making of peace – as this thoughtful book demonstrates so clearly."
George McGovern, Former United States Senator,
1972 Democratic Party nominee for President

"Dr. Dana provides a practical guide for dealing with conflict in personal relationships. He moves from scholarly content to common sense with uncommon ease."
Richard F. Celeste, Governor of Ohio

"Dr. Dana's 4-step [Self Mediation] method is elegantly simple and it works. Anyone involved with the Family Courts should be familiar with this book – whether as a layperson or as a professional."
Shelley Dickinson, J.D.
Spear & Dickinson, Hartford, Connecticut

"Managing Differences *should be required reading for all elected officials. Application of [Self Mediation] takes politics out of the 'back room, and would significantly enhance the political process."*
Harold L. "Chip" Rice, Senator (Past)
State of New Hampshire

"Managing Differences *belongs in your library."*
Mitchell P. Davis, Editor,
Directory of Experts, Authorities & Spokespersons

"You have produced a comprehensive, thorough, uncomplicated method for the lay person to manage interpersonal differences. Easily readable and understandable, it clearly presents the basic dynamics of interpersonal communication. One can maximize the potential of relationships by using this model. I highly recommend it."
Wilson (Larry) Tilley, pioneer in the human potential movement

What others say . . .

Managers & Business Leaders

"Managing Differences brings it all together – theoretically and practically. A fine guide for making our #1 problem a #1 opportunity."
Robert T. Golembiewski, Professor of Management
University of Georgia

"Excellent book. Every manager of people should read it. It is practical and will produce effective results."
Robert E. Thompson, Vice President
The Travelers Insurance Companies

"Groundbreaking! This book could become a classic."
Robert Schachat, Ph.D. President, Industrial Division,
Westchester County (New York) Psychological Association

"This is brilliant – simple, to-the-point, and immediately useful. The idea in this book has GOT to catch on."
John Nirenberg, Ph.D. Author, *Management Insight*

". . . a practical technique to empower employees to work out their differences on a direct basis."
Susan Koye, Senior Training Administrator,
McNeil Pharmaceutical (Johnson & Johnson)

"I recommend it to every employee."
Carolyn Quint Tertes, Director of Human Resources
United Cable Television

"With many years' experience in world-wide enterprises, I am impressed with the soundness and usefulness of Dr. Dana's [method] for managing people problems."
S. M. Han, President
Japan-America Foundation, Los Angeles

What others say . . .

Mediators & Dispute Resolvers

"Concise, easy to read, interesting, and factual. A manager in the 1990's either reads it now or later after problems have arisen. A must *for any professional manager."*
Richard M. Reilly, Regional Vice President,
American Arbitration Association

"Anyone engaged in day-to-day personal and professional relationships should keep Managing Differences *within easy reach."*
Wallace Warfield, Distinguished Visiting Fellow,
Administrative Conference of the United States

"Dana's book will help you apply the best of mediator techniques to your personal relationships."
Peter Lovenheim, J.D.
Author of *Mediate, Don't Litigate* (McGraw-Hill)

"Extremely well written. Excellent job of avoiding jargon."
Paul Wahrhaftig, JD, President
Conflict Resolution Center International

"User friendly, sensible. This book makes clear what can be done and how to do it."
David E. Matz, J.D., Director, Graduate Program in Dispute Resolution,
University of Massachusetts-Boston

"A no-nonsense approach to conflict management . . . a truly useful method."
Dennis P. Carey, Ph.D. Special Assistant to the Governor of Ohio on Conflict Resolution

What others say . . .

Psychotherapists & Mental Health Professionals

"Amazingly clear, concise and logical. Though easy to read, it is rich in content. There is wisdom in this book and a practical life philosophy between the lines. I could have used it sooner."
Susan M. Stine, Ph.D., M.D. Professor of Psychiatry
Yale University School of Medicine

"The most powerful and useful concepts in the social sciences are simple ideas presented clearly – a combination that occurs less often than one might imagine. Dr. Dana's 4-step [Self Mediation] method is sound, understandable, and practical. It can be mastered by the layman and can be applied in almost any interpersonal context. I have used it myself and can vouch for its effectiveness."
Graham S. Gibbard, Ph D , Clinical Professor of Psychology,
Yale University School of Medicine

". . . careful, thorough and well-balanced approach to interpersonal conflict assessment and management . . . nowhere better expressed than in this book."
James C. Miller, Ph.D.
Professor of Psychology and Director of Clinical Training
The George Washington University

"Extremely useful in day-to-day encounters."
Jose R. Gomez, Administrator, Mental Health Secretariat,
Commonwealth of Puerto Rico

"I strongly recommend this book to all who are engaged in reducing conflicts – marriage counselors, psychologists, mediators, and the general reader. It will go a long way in educating people as to how by resolving conflicts in their day-to-day lives, they can make their lives happier."
N. L. Dosajh, Ph.D., President
Indian Psychological Association (Delhi)

Managing Differences

To the heroines and heroes among us who understand that

losing is not Losing
winning is not Winning
vulnerability is not Weakness
pretending invulnerability is not Strength

May they become our leaders.

Out beyond ideas of wrongdoing and rightdoing there is a field.
I will meet you there.

~Rumi
1207 – 1273 CE
Persia (present-day Afghanistan)

Managing Differences

How to Build Better Relationships at Work and Home

Fourth Edition

Daniel Dana, Ph.D.

MTI Publications

Publisher's Cataloging-in-Publication
(Provided by Quality Books, Inc.)

Dana, Daniel.
    Managing differences : how to build better relationships at
work and home / by Daniel Dana – 4th ed.
    p. cm.
    Includes index.
    LCCN: 96-94292
    ISBN 0-9621534-5-1

    1. Mediation. 2. Interpersonal conflict. 3. Conflict
management. I. Title.

HM136.D36 1997   303.6'9
                              QBI96-40068

Published by
        MTI Publications
        5700 West 79th Street
        Prairie Village, Kansas 66208-4604
        USA

Library of Congress Catalog Card Number:
        First Edition: 88-93060

Second printing of fourth edition, July 2006
Cover design by Sean Connor
Printed in the United States of America

CONTENTS

Figures

Preface to the First Edition (1989)

Interest in conflict resolution has burgeoned in recent years. We professionals in this emerging field, like specialists in other disciplines, talk to each other a lot. We write articles, publish scientific journals, hold conventions and produce books. These efforts have created an extensive body of knowledge available to mediators and academicians.

But I fear we have lost sight of whom we are serving.

Differences in attitudes, values, priorities, lifestyles, perceptions and interests occur in every meaningful relationship – in our workplaces, families and communities. These differences often give rise to conflicts that hurt our loved ones, our organizations, and ourselves. But rarely are these conflicts brought to a mediator for resolution. We do the best we can on our own.

Where can the non-specialist turn for practical help in managing day-to-day differences with others?

This book offers a simple tool to all of us who work or live with other people. Self Mediation is not intended for mediators, consultants or researchers, although it may provide insights to their work. This tool is designed for people who do not aspire to becoming mediators, and who may not choose to bring their disputes to mediators for solution. It is for people who want more satisfaction and value from their workplace and personal relationships. It is for people who desire an alternative to coercion ("power-plays") and distancing ("walk-aways") as strategies for coping with interpersonal differences. It is for people who recognize the importance of working at relationships, and who want to prevent differences from leading to destructive conflict. Perhaps it is for you.

Bloomfield, Connecticut
December 1988

Preface to the Second Edition (1996)

Since *Managing Differences* first appeared in 1989, thousands of people have learned the 4-step Self Mediation method and applied it in their everyday lives. Owing to its publication in several languages, and its English-language distribution in Asia, Africa, and Australia, we are now confident of the cross-cultural effectiveness of this simple communication tool. And, *Managing Differences* has been adopted as a textbook for courses at colleges and universities and used as a sourcebook for corporate training and continuing education programs in North America, Europe, South Africa, and Latin America. Consequently, our understanding of how and why Self Mediation works has greatly improved in the past seven years.

The second edition of *Managing Differences* reflects this improved understanding. Several sections have been extensively revised. And, some cases are enclosed in Appendix 3 that were written by readers who provided reports about their experiences using Self Mediation and Managerial Mediation. Finally, the second edition ends with a discussion of "Common Courtesy," pointing the way toward even more "user friendly" mediation tools for everyday life.

So it is my hope that the second edition constitutes an even more valuable resource to empower even more people to act proactively in improving the important relationships in their lives – at work and home. The past success and the future promise of this practical communication tool reaffirms my commitment to a career of helping people realize the potential of their relationships, making their organizations more effective, their communities more satisfying, and their lives more fulfilling.

Phoenix, Arizona
February 1996

Preface to the Revised Second Edition (1997)

This revision is prompted by two developments.

First, *Talk It Out: Four Steps to Managing People Problems in Your Organization,* a version of the first edition published by Human Resource Development Press in 1990, has been replaced by *Managing Differences* as the sourcebook for a wide range of corporate and organizational training courses on resolving conflict in the workplace. So, the chapter on "Managing cultural differences," which had been written specifically for *Talk It Out,* is now included as Appendix 4.

Second, the *Managing Differences LearningTest,* the core component of a leaderless staff training program for managing conflict at work, has been developed in a broad range of customized versions. An editorial revision was needed to make *Managing Differences* more suitable as its sourcebook.

Aside from these two developments, *Managing Differences* continues to serve superbly as the sourcebook for Self Mediation, which is increasingly recognized as not only a core competency for the workplace, but also as an empowering life-skill for us all.

Overland Park, Kansas
July 1997

Preface to the Third Edition (2001)

The four years since publication of the revised second edition have brought remarkable developments:

1. The *Self-as-Mediator Seminar,* which is the learning program in which people learn to apply the communication tool described in this book, now rivals the *Manager-as-Mediator Seminar* in popularity. *Managing Differences* now serves as the sourcebook for both seminars.
2. To accommodate the support materials accompanying the *Self-as-Mediator Seminar,* the tool has been renamed Self Mediation.
3. Website www.mediationworks.com, which is the home on the Internet of the Mediation Training Institute, has become perhaps the most frequently visited mediation-related site on the world-wide web.
4. Certified Trainers of Workplace Mediation, who draw upon the contents of this book, now bring its message to people and organizations on six continents, in English and in Spanish.
5. *Conflict Resolution: Mediation Tools for Everyday Worklife* (McGraw-Hill, 2001) extends the insights of *Managing Differences* to managerial mediation, preventive mediation, team mediation, and the strategic management of organizational conflict.

Still, the message of *Managing Differences* remains essentially unchanged. It continues a sturdy and reliable vehicle for helping people build better relationships at work and home, worldwide.

Prairie Village, Kansas
September 2001

Preface to the Fourth Edition (2005)

Coincidentally, the third edition was published the month the world changed – September 2001. Our paradigm of conflict and its resolution suddenly shifted. We live in a less innocent age.

Like so many millions of other innocents, I was stunned into near-paralysis by the attack of September 11. For several days, I could hardly muster the enthusiasm to do my daily work of teaching and advocating conflict resolution. It seemed so tiny, so puny, so insignificant.

Eventually, my existential choice became clear, as it must for everyone beset by huge, irrecoverable loss: Do I choose to live, or do I choose to die? I can do nothing about terrorism on a global scale, but I can still do my work of interpersonal peacemaking, however tiny. So can we all.

Managing Differences continues to serve as the sourcebook for learning by ever-greater numbers of people who participate in the Managing Differences Seminar Series. Once again, I feel my work to be important. So is yours.

Prairie Village, Kansas
November 2004

Preview of . . .

Self Mediation
A 4-Step Method for Building Better Relationships

Step 1: **FIND A TIME TO TALK**
The **Approach**
The **Issue Statement**
The **Request**
The **Sale** (if needed)
The **Cardinal Rules** (if needed)
The **Time & Place**

Step 2: **PLAN THE CONTEXT**
Removing the "land mines" from your environment.

Step 3: **TALK IT OUT**
The **Opening**
Express appreciation
Express optimism
Reminders: *The Cardinal Rules*
State the issue
The **Invitation**
The **Dialogue**
Task #1: Stay engaged in the *Essential Process*
Task #2: Support *Conciliatory Gestures*
The **Breakthrough**
When these TASKS are performed during this special
DIALOGUE in an appropriate CONTEXT, partners'
attitudes can shift from "me-against-you" to "us-
against-the-problem." This shift opens a window of
opportunity for making a Deal that is good for both
people.
Step 4: **MAKE A DEAL**
Balanced
Behaviorally specific
Written

This practical peacemaking tool may be used by *everyone* – *not* just specialists in mediation and conflict resolution.

The dispute resolution profession may have lost sight of the obvious fact that most people who strive to build better relationships at work and home do it on their own, without professional assistance. The "Self Mediation" method has been carefully developed and tested so it can be used by non-professionals. The mediator's tool kit has been emptied of all unessential, special-purpose, nice-to-know tools. Only the basics remain here, in this general-purpose tool for the non-specialist.

The intent of this book is to offer you a simple, effective communication tool for managing differences in relationships that matter to you. I will have failed in my mission if after reading it you say to yourself, "Okay, sounds good, but it's too complicated for me to use." Learning this method alone will not make you an expert mediator or negotiator. But using it can empower you to build better relationships at work and home. Make Self Mediation, and its underlying insights about interpersonal conflict, your routine response when troubling differences arise. Others will thank you for doing so!

A Word on Words

Special Terms

A few key concepts are central to the message in this book, so it is important that I communicate them effectively. To do so, I will use words and phrases that have designated meanings. These are listed below as a special vocabulary, with the page number where each term first appears. Note that some of these terms differ somewhat from their familiar definitions.

Terms that have special meanings will appear with the first letters capitalized to distinguish them from everyday speech. Each term will be defined when it first appears in the text. You will also find full definitions in the Glossary.

List continues on next page

---

[1] The communication tool that constitutes the core message of this book is called "Self Mediation" in the third edition. It was referred to as "Do-it-yourself Mediation" in the second edition, and the "4-Step Method" in the first edition.

[2] Called "Non-communication" in the first edition.

[3] Called "Power-play" in the first edition.

Toward Non-sexist Language

The evolution of the English language has left today's writers with a troublesome legacy – we have no common-gender singular personal pronouns.

The reader is no doubt familiar with the various ways that authors address this problem – using generic masculine or feminine pronouns, combined terms ("he/she" and "her/him"), and pluralizing all pronouns ("they" and "them"). For various ethical and practical reasons, I am uncomfortable with these solutions.

In this book, I will alternate masculine and feminine gender pronouns from paragraph to paragraph, or from scenario to scenario. By alerting you in advance, I hope to minimize any distraction of your attention from the book's message that alternating genders may cause.

Part 1

THE CHALLENGE

Chapter 1:

INTERPERSONAL TRAGEDIES:
Why the World Needs a Simple, Practical Peacemaking Tool
for Everyday Life

Seamus and Susan work together. Or, we should say
they are *supposed* to work together. If their manager really knew
how little work got done, she would have a fit. Their jobs
require that they cooperate, but Seamus finds cooperation
impossible under the circumstances. It seems that every time he
tries to get Susan to do her share of the work, she finds some
new excuse. Seamus winds up taking work home and spending
extra hours doing what Susan is supposed to do. He's fed up.
Last weekend Seamus updated his resume and made some calls

to friends in other companies. He decided he doesn't need to take this grief any longer.

Hayden tries to remember what it was she admired about Oliver before they married. Whatever those redeeming qualities were, they seem to have vanished. Oh sure, Oliver is a pleasant fellow, and her friends say he's charming. It's hard to know what the real problem is – they argue about money, about parenting roles, even about which TV show to watch. Lately, they've been avoiding each other, trying not to spark another fight. Whatever the problem, Hayden is becoming discouraged. This is not what she wanted from marriage.

The Scope of the Problem

These are not soap opera scenarios. They are only two of the millions of real-life dramas played out daily. The world is teeming with interpersonal tragedies like these.

"Tragedy" is a strong word, but Seamus and Hayden are strongly affected. Workplace conflicts lead to stagnated careers, job stress, lowered productivity, lessened motivation – even termination and resignation. Emotional alienation in families leads to unrewarding marriages, troubled children, distant relationships – even divorce, abandonment, and sometimes violence.

Three million involuntary job terminations and over 800,000 voluntary resignations occur each year in the United States – figures on the rise in this age of "downsizing." How many of these departures broke a potentially productive bond between employee and employer? Over one million couples divorce each year in this country alone. Did all that love really disappear? Human nature drives us to *seek* relationships, not to leave them.

For every terminated relationship, there are many more in which partners maintain a tense and distant truce that brings them only meager satisfaction. Chronic unresolved interpersonal conflicts cause needless emotional pain and wastefully drain individual vitality and organizational resources. And, the United States represents only one-twentieth of the world's population. The magnitude of loss, in human and financial terms, is incalculable.

Tragedy Can Be Averted

So many of these tragedies are achingly unnecessary. There exists a way for individuals in strained relationships to take charge of managing differences and resolving conflicts. They can regain trust and intimacy, and resume teamwork. The method is so simple it may seem simplistic. Yet it has the power to transform conflict into cooperation, mistrust into trust, and alienation into meaningful human connectedness. It harnesses natural forces lying dormant within relationships that can heal wounds caused by anger, insult, and hurt – the carnage of mutual revenge.

Differences, Needs, and Conflict

In every relationship, the differences that make us unique individuals are also sources of potential conflict between us. We differ in our values, self-interests, priorities, and in many other ways. The greater the differences, the heavier the burden on our ability to manage those differences. The less effectively we manage differences, the more conflict we experience as a result.

Relationships satisfy needs. Whether at work or home, every important relationship is a vehicle for delivering value to each partner. Our relationships with our bosses hold potential for satisfying our needs to feel productive, to accomplish meaningful work, to produce widgets, and to earn paychecks. Marriages and other intimate relationships can satisfy our needs for emotional and physical contact, for security, and for fulfillment of our identities as women and men. When our needs are met, we are satisfied, happy people.

Conflict drains the capacity of relationships to satisfy our needs. When we experience too much unresolved conflict, the relationship loses its ability to satisfy us. We are left alone, isolated, unable to do by ourselves what requires two to do.

Ironically, as we depend more heavily on a relationship to satisfy our needs, conflict is more likely to occur. High interdependency can cause conflict to grow more intense. Yet, to paraphrase poet John Donne, "No one is an island." Human nature and the human condition require that we depend on others, that we be interdependent with others in satisfying our individual needs.

Room for Improvement

Interpersonal differences that breed the conflicts, and the tragedies, that each of us experiences from time to time can be better managed. No matter how skilled we are now, potential exists for us to be happier and more productive. In this book a practical method for managing differences is introduced that eliminates the use of Distancing ("Walk-aways") and Coercion ("Power-plays") – the typical yet counterproductive ways of coping with difficult situations. You can use Self Mediation to build better relationships at work and at home.

A Personal Need

As author, my relationship with you, the reader, holds the potential for satisfying my need to feel that I am a useful human being, that the time I devote to my chosen career makes a meaningful contribution to others. In this book, I offer you what I know about turning interpersonal conflict into interpersonal peace. I would be gratified to learn that Self Mediation has helped you. Let me hear your story. Write to me in care of the publisher.

Chapter 2:

DOES SELF-HELP HELP?
How This Book Might Save
Your Job, Your Marriage, Your . . .

Often, while reading self-help books, I think to myself, "It sounds good, but I doubt I will remember much of this a month from now." I am skeptical of suggestions that a quick dose of advice will have long-term impact in real-life situations.

The Problem of Self-control

Much of the advice in self-help books urges us to alter our perceptions, thoughts, beliefs, motives, intentions, attitudes, or values. Once these changes are accomplished, it is suggested, then some personal problem related to the subject of the book will be solved. Perhaps so.

My skepticism lies in the difficulty of accomplishing these changes. Perceptions, thoughts, attitudes, and the like are invisible "mental events" that occur privately within our heads. They are not observable by others. Mental events are extremely difficult to control or manipulate. Uncomfortable feelings, unwanted thoughts, disturbing perceptions, and self-destructive motives can intrude, despite our efforts at self-control. For most of us, our willpower is seldom adequate to fend off the challenge of strong, persistent thoughts and feelings.

Behavior is easier to control than mental activity. Behavioral events are observable and can be controlled by the behaver. Behavior can be described in concrete terms, like a physical object can be described. We can say, "I'm going to write that report, even though I don't want to." The writing is behavior; the wanting to is a mental event. Behavior can be seen or heard. Precisely defined behavior either is or it isn't; it happens or it doesn't happen. We may dispute the motives that give rise to the behavior, but the fact of its occurrence is indisputable.

An Illustration

The United States government has been attempting for decades to eradicate racism from American society. Critics have faulted the effort on the grounds that it is impossible to "legislate morality." In other words, they argue that some citizens will hold prejudicial attitudes toward people of other races regardless of laws to the contrary. The critics have a point. In truth, racism is a category of mental events happening in people's heads that cannot be *directly* affected by commandments that they not exist. A moment of introspection will corroborate this point: Many of us who grew up in racially divided communities learned racist attitudes that we now are trying to sweep from the dusty corners of our minds. Despite our best intentions, we struggle against the effects of decades of socialization to eliminate unwanted traces of racial prejudice.

With a 1971 US Supreme Court decision, the federal government spurred the busing of students to achieve racial integration in schools. The busing program makes no pretense of directly altering students' attitudes toward people of other races. It simply requires that students of different races spend time together. We know for a fact that when young people frequently interact in multiracial environments, their attitudes change. So the Supreme Court decision was directed at a change in behavior, not in personal beliefs or values. However, by busing students (behavioral events), the government is *indirectly* affecting racism (mental events).

Behavioral Prescription

This book offers no prescriptions about how you should think or feel in interpersonal conflict. As an adult, your mental events have been largely fixed through decades of life experience. Admittedly, our patterns of thinking and feeling can be changed, but probably not by simply reading this or any other self-help book. That is the task of psychotherapy and other more intensive paths to personal growth.

Self Mediation is a *behavioral* prescription, a 4-step recipe consisting of behavioral ingredients. When its directions are followed, the recipe can indirectly change how you and your Other* *feel* (reduced anger, increased trust), what *attitudes* you have (increased optimism about your relationship and your ability to cooperate), and your *intentions* toward each other (less hostile, more friendly).

---

* The term "Other" with a capital "O" will be used in this book when referring to the other person in our two-person, ongoing, interdependent relationships.

Link Between Behavior and Attitude

The link between the busing program's behavioral ingredients and the resulting changes in racial attitudes may not be obvious. Just how and why does a behavioral event change a mental event in a predictable way? That is where behavioral science enters the picture. Contrary to critics' claims that busing does not change children's racial attitudes, scientific research has demonstrated clearly that, given enough time, forced integration of schools does in fact change children's attitudes, reducing their negative racial stereotypes.

The link between the behavioral ingredients in the recipe of Self Mediation and the interpersonal harmony that it produces may not be obvious either. Just how and why does communicating as this simple tool prescribes result in reduced conflict, increased trust, and better teamwork? Part 5 of this book is dedicated to explaining this link.

But Self Mediation is not simply untested theory, to be taken on faith. Its effectiveness has been demonstrated consistently. It works even if you are skeptical, and it works even if you don't understand why it works. It is only necessary that you make the deliberate choice to use this communication tool as it is designed to be used. The cases in Appendix 3 tell stories about how readers of the first edition of *Managing Differences* used it in real life.

How *This* Self-help Book Can Help

So, this book's central purpose is not to give the reader self-insight or to label communication styles. Rather, it offers you very practical, concrete, behaviorally specific advice for managing differences that can erupt in destructive conflict, eroding the value of your important relationships.

Wherever you are as you read these words, you live and work with other people. I invite you to test Self Mediation for yourself. Use it just once in a relationship that matters to you. Then watch the results. Notice how trust is regained, affection is renewed, and cooperative work is resumed. Then continue to use this simple communication tool to get more satisfaction from living and working with Others.

Chapter 3:

ASSESSING THE COST OF CONFLICT
IN YOUR ORGANIZATION*

NOTE IN FOURTH EDITION, 2005: The assessment method in this chapter (now titled the *Dana Measure of Financial Cost of Organizational Conflict)* is available as an on-line cost-of-conflict calculator available to the public at www.mediationworks.com.

Unmanaged employee conflict is perhaps the largest reducible cost in organizations today – and probably the least recognized.

It is estimated that over 65% of performance problems result from strained relationships between employees – not from deficits in individual employees' skill or motivation.

Interdependent workplace relationships are a fertile soil from which conflict can sprout. Organizations are lush gardens hosting many flourishing varieties of this annoying and resource-sapping weed.

* This chapter is adapted from an article that first appeared as "The Costs of Organizational Conflict" in *Organization Development Journal,* Fall 1984.

Now let's look at how this weed saps financial health and vitality. This chapter can be used as a self-administered instrument.* Use the worksheet at the end of this chapter with the following instructions to calculate the strictly financial costs that a particular conflict incurs, aside from its impact on quality of worklife and job satisfaction.

Worksheet Instructions

First, identify one conflict that is very familiar to you, either by having been a participant or a close observer. It may be a conflict that is still current, or one that happened in the past. Jot down a key word or phrase to help you stay targeted on that particular conflict.

The "cost factors" listed on the worksheet are the primary ways that conflict incurs financial costs. Not all cost factors are relevant to every conflict, but every conflict incurs cost by several of these means. Analyze your targeted conflict by asking yourself, with regard to each cost factor in turn, "Did/does the conflict I am analyzing have the effect of . . . . . . " If you answer yes, calculate its dollar cost in the ways suggested, and enter your estimate in the space provided. When you are completed, sum the column to derive an estimated total cost.

* A revised and updated instrument, *The Dana Measure of Financial Costs of Organizational Conflict,* is available free at www.mediationworks.com. A team-oriented version of the instrument also appears as "Measuring the Cost of Team Conflict" in *The 1996 Best Practices for Teams,* edited by Glenn Parker, published by Human Resource Development Press.

Factor 1: Wasted time

Invariably, conflict distracts employees from otherwise productive use of their time. A classic management study* revealed that up to 30% of a typical manager's time is spent dealing with conflict. A more current study** of practicing managers showed that 42% of their time is spent reaching agreements with others when conflicts occur.

Estimate the amount of time wasted by each person who is/was affected by the team conflict. Then calculate the financial cost as a fraction of monthly or annual salary or wage, including the value of insurance and other fringe benefits (typically at least 50% of gross salary).

For example, let's say each of four employees wasted 40 hours during a six month period because conflict disrupted their work And, let's say the annual salary of each employee is $40,000. Forty hours is one week of work time, which is one-fifty-second of one year's salary. A year's salary is generally about two-thirds of total compensation. So, the dollar value of the four employees' wasted time is $4615.38.

Factor 2: Reduced decision quality

Decisions made under conditions of conflict are always inferior to decisions made when cooperation prevails. This is

---

* "A Survey of Managerial Interests with Respect to Conflict" by Kenneth W. Thomas and W. H. Schmidt, *Academy of Management Journal,* June 1976.

** "Managers as Negotiators" by Carol Watson and Richard Hoffman, *Leadership Quarterly,* 7(1), 1996.

true for two reasons. First, we know that good decisions must be based on an optimum quantity and quality of objective information. If information is withheld or distorted by those who are depended upon to provide it (which nearly always happens when information providers are in conflict with the decision-maker), then the decision cannot be the best one possible.

Second, if conflict is present between people who share decision-making authority, as in the case of team-based decisions, the resulting decisions are likely to be contaminated by the power struggles between those people. A precise estimate of cost is probably impossible. But ask yourself, "What opportunities were lost by poor decisions that were affected by this conflict, and what might have been gained if a better decision had been made?"

Considering these influences on decisions made by the people affected by your target conflict, estimate their cost and put the figure on the line provided. Place a conservative (i.e., on the low side of the range of its potential financial impact) figure there, even though the actual cost may be highly variable and very uncertain. Guideline: 50% of the dollar impact of decisions that were made while the conflict was going on (e.g., estimate $2500 if a team was disputing whether to purchase a $5000 piece of equipment.)

Factor 3: Loss of skilled employees

Organizations invest in employees' skills by paying a premium salary upon hiring and by providing training thereafter. Exit interviews, which ascertain reasons for terminations, reveal that chronic unresolved conflict acts as a decisive factor in at least 50% of all such departures. Conflict accounts for up to 90% of involuntary departures, with the probable exception of staff reductions due to downsizing and restructuring. Raytheon Corporation determined that replacing an engineer costs 150% of his/her total annual compensation. This determination was reached by accounting for lost productivity, recruiting fees, interviewing time, staffing department employee salaries, orientation and retraining costs, etc. So, replacing an employee whose annual salary is $40,000 incurs a cost of $90,000. If one or more employees departed at least partially because of the conflict you are analyzing, figure the cost to your organization.

For example, using conservative estimates, let's say that one employee voluntarily resigned, and that his/her decision to leave was only 50% due to the conflict. Using Raytheon's figures, the dollar cost of this factor is half of $90,000, or $45,000.

Factor 4: Restructuring

Often, design of workflow is altered in an attempt to reduce the amount of interaction required between employees in conflict. Unfortunately, the restructured work is usually less efficient than the original design, which would have been satisfactory if the conflicting employees had been able to work together. As with Factor 2 above, it is impossible to precisely calculate the resulting inefficiency, but your subjective assessment will give a reasonable estimate. Again, be sure to enter a conservative (low side) figure on your worksheet. Guideline: 10% of the combined salaries of employees whose relationship was restructured for the time the restructuring is in effect. Example: Estimate $8000 if four employees, each of whom is paid $40,000 annually, were reassigned to different task groups for a six month period, i.e., (($40,000 X 4)/10)/2). Rationale: The financial value of employees (i.e., "human resources") to an employer for performing specified work is, by definition, roughly equivalent to their salaries. If that work must later be restructured to control interpersonal conflict, the redesigned work relationship is probably not the most efficient allocation of the human resources.

Factor 5: Sabotage/theft/damage

Studies reveal a direct correlation between prevalence of employee conflict and the amount of damage and theft of inventory and equipment. And, covert sabotage of work processes and of management's efforts usually occurs when employees are angry at their employer. Much of the cost incurred by this factor is hidden from management's view, excused as "accidental" or "inadvertent" errors. This cost is almost certainly greater than you may realize. Again, enter a conservative figure on the worksheet. Guideline: 10% of the acquisition cost of equipment, tools, and supplies that conflicted employees use in performing their jobs. Example: $2500, if an operator of a $20,000 machine in a manufacturing environment is angry toward his/her supervisor ($2000 for careless operation and maintenance of the machine, plus $500 for unnecessary scrap and waste of raw materials).

Factor 6: Lowered job motivation

From time to time, most employees experience erosion of job motivation due to the stress of trying to get along with a "difficult person." As a baseline figure, use the productivity that would have occurred had no conflict occurred. Then, estimate a percentage decline of that productivity. Multiply that percentage times the dollar value of the total compensation of the person(s) affected to derive a figure for Factor 6.

For example, let's say that the productivity of three employees was eroded by 20% for a period of three months.

Using figures similar to those above, the three employees' total compensation was 3 X $60,000, or $180,000. Since one-fourth of this amount ($45,000) was earned during the three month period, the conflict cost the organization $9000.

Factor 7: Lost work time

Absenteeism has been shown to correlate with job stress, especially the stress associated with anger toward co-workers. This stress, combined with disregard for how one's absence impacts others, leads to employees' choosing to take time off – sometimes excused as a "sick day." And, medical science has determined that nearly every physical illness and injury, from viral infections to cancer to workplace accidents, are partially "psychogenic." That is, they are caused in part by psychological or emotional conditions. The portion of lost work time that has resulted from your targeted conflict is largely hidden from your direct view, with the possible exception of your own absences. Still, you can arrive at an estimate by prorating daily or monthly compensation. Again, be sure to enter a conservative estimate on your worksheet. Guideline: 10% of annual salaries of employees in conflict. Example: $18,000 if all six members of a department, each of whom is paid $25,000 annually, are in ongoing conflict with their supervisor, who is paid $30,000, throughout the year
($25,000 X 6) : 10 + $30,000 ÷ 10.

Factor 8: Health costs

As mentioned under Factor 7, illnesses and injuries requiring medical attention are partially psychogenic, and conflict contributes to their psychogenesis. Since the rate of claims affects the premium paid by an employer to its insurer, insurance is an indirect cost of workplace conflict. Estimate the percentage of the psychogenic component of medical problems that have occurred while your targeted conflict has gone on, and multiply this percentage times the premium increase imposed by your organization's insurer. Admittedly, this psychogenic component is difficult to ascertain, and you may not be privy to the insurance costs of your employer. So, enter a conservative figure based on your knowledge of these matters. A shortcut is to enter 10% of the number you have entered for Factor 6, "lowered job motivation," since the stress that results in reduced productivity is also related to our physical health.

What is the total cost?

Now add the figures in each of the eight cost factors to derive an estimated total cost of your targeted conflict. Remember, this accounts for the cost of just *one* conflict – how many others have occurred in your organization if you extend your estimate over the period of a year?

By repeating the analysis for other conflicts, or by multiplying the resulting figure by the number of conflicts that have occurred, we gain fuller appreciation of conflict as an expensive organizational process.

If you are a manager, enabling your employees to use Self Mediation may be the best decision you can make today.

Cost Estimation Worksheet

Key word/phrase to identify a conflict: _____

<u>COST FACTORS</u>   <u>ESTIMATED COST</u>

1) Wasted time $_____
   - salary/benefits per hour/day (150%)

2) Reduced decision quality $_____
   - any decision made by you and/or others,
     independently or jointly, affected by the conflict

3) Loss of skilled employees $_____
   - cost of loss of human resource (150% of total
     annual compensation)

4) Restructuring $_____
   - Inefficiency of work redesigned to accommodate
     conflict

5) Sabotage/theft/damage $_____
   - equipment, work processes, reputations

6) Lowered job motivation $_____
   - reduced performance/productivity
   - % reduction times salary

7) Lost work time $_____
   - # of days lost at prorated daily salary

8) Health costs $_____
   - stress related
   - insurance premiums linked to rate of claims

                                                _____

            TOTAL COST: $_____

Chapter 4:

WHY DO WE SELF-DESTRUCT?

In win-lose conflict, I hurt myself as much as I hurt my Other. Why do I find it so difficult to approach my Other in a both-gain* spirit?

A few key obstacles impair our ability to manage differences in ongoing interdependent relationships at work and home. These obstacles fall into two categories: "Wrong Reflexes" and "Illusions." Together, they account for much of our puzzling human tendency to behave self-destructively, to persist in win-lose struggles that damage our own self-interests.

* The expression "both-gain" is used rather than the more familiar term "win-win" to avoid the connotation of competition that is inherent to "winning." By implication, if there is a winner, there must also be a loser. The intent of this book is to suggest that both participants can gain – without losing and without defeating the Other.

We seem unable to learn a better way, despite a multitude of prior episodes in any lifetime that can only be termed failures to manage differences well.

Wrong Reflexes

The Way We Were

Our evolutionary legacy haunts us. In simpler times, before humans lived in communities larger than a few dozen, when organizations as workplaces had not yet been invented, and before humanistic values had developed, our reflexes served us well. In those times, it was adaptive to act on two assumptions:

1) that the best way to avoid danger was to escape, to remove ourselves from the presence of the threat,

2) and that, if escape were blocked, the best way to protect ourselves from a threat was to meet force with force in the hope of defeating the Other.

This pair of automatic assumptions is popularly known as the "flight or fight" instinct.

These reflexes were very adaptive for our pre-historic ancestors. The extent to which they were functioning determined how successfully the individual survived each day's life-threatening crises, and had another opportunity to pass genetic characteristics on to descendants. In other words, these automatic responses in dangerous situations eventually became instinctive, part of our biological nature. Today, we are the descendants in an unbroken chain of millions of generations of individuals who survived the dangers long enough to procreate.

We are the result of natural selection pressures that favored
individuals who had what are, in modern life, "Wrong Reflexes."

Times Have Changed

Why are these reflexes wrong today when they were
right in the past? Much has changed. Today, the dangers posed
by our co-workers, family, and friends are seldom physical
threats. Escape (flight) is a costly option, since we are in long
term interdependent relationships. We must go to our jobs
tomorrow and work with the same people, then come home to
the same spouse. Resolving a conflict by terminating these
relationships is a drastic measure.

The alternative reflex, using force to defeat the opponent
(fight), is no better. Physical assault is not acceptable in our
culture as a means of dealing with people who differ from us.
Threats, intimidation, and coercive force to win our way may
succeed in the short run. But such tactics lay the groundwork for
future retaliation by the other person. Coercion is a self-defeating
tactic for handling differences in ongoing interdependent
relationships – those that matter most at work and home.

But our bodies don't know that anything has changed
since we lived in caves. Our genetic code, including the genes
that control these behavioral mechanisms, is nearly identical to
that of the individuals whose two million year old fossils are
being unearthed in east Africa. Our reflexes – the ones we
inherited from our survivor ancestors – still prompt us to act as if
we are confronting a tiger on the plains of the ancient continent
of Pangaea. We still reflexively interpret each confrontation as a
win-lose encounter, where only one of us can win and the other
must lose. We still reflexively respond to threats by trying to
withdraw or escape from interaction. When trapped and escape
is blocked, we still draw upon our resources to try to coerce the

other into submission or compliance. This reaction is *not* conscious, and it *is* universal. Every biologically normal human being responds this way.

Modern Forms

Of course, we no longer fight with spears and flee into the forest. We use updated forms of those ancient impulses. Physical attack has been replaced by tactics like cutting off funds, overriding objections, and stating ultimatums. Physical flight has been replaced by avoiding meetings, failing to return phone calls, and watching television.

Now that we have evolved that most-human vehicle of language to express ourselves, we have developed a curious hybrid of fight and flight, "passive aggression." Popular forms of passive aggression include making uncomplimentary remarks to associates about the Other, covertly undermining support of her projects, and finding excuses for not responding to a request. Having language enables us to inflict harm on the Other from a safe distance, concealing our aggressive motives.

Disguised in modern forms, our ancient impulses are still very much with us. These Wrong Reflexes are the two and only two means of coping with conflict that our instinct-driven bodies allow us to recognize:

> 1) **Distancing** ("flight"), an effort to withdraw from perceived threat – also called "Walk-aways"

> 2) **Coercion** ("fight"), an effort to defeat the Other – also called "Power-plays"

Illusions

Illusions are distorted perceptions that do not convey accurate information about the "external world," as philosophers refer to all that is outside our skin. Our behavior is based on the assumption that our perceptions are accurate. A person who believes that he is an alien from Jupiter who is being persecuted by the CIA is behaving reasonably and appropriately – assuming it is true that he is actually an alien from Jupiter and is being persecuted by the CIA. Perception is the process of interpreting the external world so that we may act in it.

Whose Truth is True?

Perceptions are illusions when they are inaccurate interpretations of reality. But how do we know if our perceptions are accurate? When psychiatrists say they are inaccurate, we label the problem "mental illness." When our co-worker or spouse says they are inaccurate, we call the problem "conflict."

We generally accept majority-rule as a way of deciding what is external reality. That is, if most people say something is true, then it must be true. However, this way of deciding about reality is imperfect. The majority of Europeans believed the world was flat until fifteenth-century explorers discovered that we can go to the East by sailing West.

In interpersonal conflicts, we have only two versions of the truth to choose between – yours and mine – and we may vigorously debate whose version is the correct one. Appeals for support by majority-rule ("everyone agrees with me, just ask around") seldom succeed in convincing the Other to accept the correctness of our position. Employing coercive tactics – Power-plays – to "win" the conflict between your truth and mine, especially when there is no mutually acceptable independent arbiter, may make us feel good for as long as we imagine that we are winning. But it also undermines our own interests – we squander any support and value that the relationship might have had for us. So, to the degree that we harm our own interests, we self-destruct.

Illusions are universal – that is, they occur in everyone. So, we cannot claim that they result from the Other's psychological problems. They are normal, an integral part of our biological perceptual mechanisms – we are simply built that way.

Three illusions shed especially revealing light on how we self-destruct in interpersonal conflict:

> The *"Win-Lose Illusion"*
> The *"Bad Person Illusion"*
> The *"Boulder-in-the-Road Illusion"*

The Win-Lose Illusion

Our needs are fundamentally incompatible;
only one of us can prevail.

Some authors urge us to appreciate that conflict provides a valuable opportunity for creative problem-solving, synergy, and personal growth. My chosen career is conflict resolution, and I am regarded by some as an expert in the field. Lapsing into a moment of candor, I disclose to you now that I personally have great difficulty, while engaged in conflict, staying mindful of these virtues. Like other fallible human beings, I initially react to conflicts as if they are win-lose situations. My Other and I argue different positions on an issue, and I assume that the incompatibility of our needs means that the outcome must necessarily favor one of us over the other. Pending calmer reflection, I assume that only one of us can be right, only one of us can get what we want – the other must lose. Only with great mental effort can I imagine the possibility that neither of us must lose, that a both-gain outcome is available to us. Until then, the possibility of a both-gain outcome does not enter my view of the realm of possibilities. The illusion is that a win-lose outcome is inevitable when, in fact, both-gain alternatives nearly always exist.

I don't believe I am unique in this odd blindness. Nor do I believe that transcending the Win-Lose Illusion is easy. Nor, I'm afraid, is clear vision of both-gain possibilities within the reach of the vast majority of us. I believe it is a futile exercise to suggest that we educate the population of the planet to recognize the possibility of both-gain outcomes to our interpersonal conflicts. That would be swimming upstream a torrent of biological imperatives.

But all is not gloom. It may be true that the Win-Lose Illusion will regularly blind us as we struggle to manage differences with others day-to-day. Happily, however, success in using Self Mediation does not require that either you or your Other is able to avoid this troublesome trickster of perception.

The Bad Person Illusion

Our conflict is the direct result
of your incompetence, ignorance, meanness,
or other defect;
it can only be resolved if
you recognize and correct your defects.

When we have managed our differences poorly – that is, by means of the Wrong Reflexes – certain attitudes about our Other become entrenched over time and seem absolutely correct. We grow to think that he is bad in some way – mean, corrupt, immoral, malicious, stupid. In our more generous moments, we may kindly offer the concession that the Other's behavior is due to being simply crazy or disturbed, suggesting that she is not fully in control of her behavior.

By believing that the conflict is a direct consequence of our Other's personal defects, we are able to absolve ourselves of responsibility for contributing to the problem. We comfort ourselves with the belief that the other person is at fault, and that we are innocent, hapless victims.

A Two-Way Street

But notice a curious fact about the Bad Person Illusion: It is almost always *reciprocal.* That is, each participant believes the *other* is at fault. The regularity of the Bad Person Illusion being a two-way street suggests that it may not be true that one of the persons is in fact evil or crazy. To believe that the cause of our conflict lies in inherently bad personal characteristics of the Other is a distortion of reality – the cause is *differentness,* not badness.

Let's assume for a moment that our Other is indeed bad. Does acting on that value judgment lead us toward resolution? Since he probably feels quite the same about us, holding us in low esteem as we do him, he is not likely to accept our judgment and acquiesce to our positions on the disputed issues. So, insisting that the Other accept blame simply doesn't work, regardless of how sure we are of his faults or even of how correct our perceptions are. Negotiations in an atmosphere of Bad Person judgments only lead to impasse.

Former President Jimmy Carter was criticized by some for treating military leader, General Raoul Cedras, as a legitimate player during his successful mediation to resolve the crisis in Haiti in 1995. The national consensus was that Gen. Cedras was simply a cruel dictator, undeserving of the legitimacy and respect shown him by President Carter. But Carter wisely appealed to the military leader's "sense of honor, sense of dignity." He knew that people don't want to participate in problem-solving dialogue when you insult them. Carter's mediation succeeded because he steadfastly focused on the need for reconciliation, avoiding the temptation of treating Cedras as a Bad Person.*

Self-fulfilling Prophesy

Over the course of a chronic conflict, the Bad Person belief may seem to come true. Our self-protective, defensive behavior provokes the Other into exhibiting "bad" behavior – just as her retaliatory behavior provokes us. Under the stress of the moment, we may act crazy, stupid, or mean – we do "bad" things. So, the illusion becomes a self-fulfilling prophesy.

But even when we behave cruelly or senselessly, we justify our own "bad" behavior as resulting from having been mercilessly provoked by the Other. We insist that it is atypical of us to act that way, whereas the bad behavior exhibited by the Other reveals deep flaws in her personality. We find it difficult to regard the Other's behavior in that same, understanding light.

The Bad Person Illusion, then, is the distorted image that the Other's behavior derives from his flawed character. His behavior is not interpreted, as is more often the case, as a natural, normal response to the conflict between us. Even when there is some majority-rule support that our version of reality is correct, such as a psychiatrist's diagnosis, the illusion still plays a role. It causes us to exaggerate the difference between us and our Other in terms of how justifiable and situation-dependent the "bad" behaviors are. That is, we excuse ourselves but are unable to excuse our Other.

* *The Carter Center News*, July 24, 1995.

An Illustration*

It may be difficult for many readers to refrain from applying the Bad Person Illusion to the former apartheid government of South Africa. How could a fair-minded and reasonable person not regard the oppression of millions of people through enforcement of discriminatory and dehumanizing laws as anything other than evil? Would we not all agree that the leaders of the apartheid regime were either evil or crazy or both? Were they not "bad people?"

Interestingly, adherents of apartheid have held a quite reciprocal perception. Many supporters of the previous regime no doubt regarded black people negatively – as uncivilized, unintelligent, untrustworthy – as "bad people." And yet, by any conventional diagnosis of mental health, these adherents were not "insane." And, since they loved their children and families, had sincere and meaningful friendships, and cared about the well-being of others, were they "evil?" Although it may strain our objectivity to do so, we must acknowledge that supporters of apartheid behaved reasonably and appropriately within the context of their system of values and perception of the world.

So the great social conflict of South Africa exemplifies a reciprocal perception that the other side is by its nature, evil – the Bad Person Illusion on a national scale.

* This illustration is adapted from text prepared for the South African edition of *Managing Differences,* published by William Waterman Publications, Rivonia, South Africa, 1995.

Designed to achieve interpersonal, not national, peace, Self Mediation is surely inadequate for resolving a conflict of such magnitude. Nevertheless, in hindsight we can see that the apartheid policy of non-communication with black leaders, which rested largely on the perception of their being "bad people," precluded the possibility of genuine resolution, just as the Wrong Reflex of Distancing from relationship has that same effect on prospects for interpersonal peace.

Is the Bad Person Illusion a fatal flaw of human nature that makes it impossible for us to manage our differences constructively? Fortunately not. Using Self Mediation does not require that we or our Others be able to free ourselves from this most human perceptual trap. We have the power to *choose* to communicate, even when our perceptions are contaminated by the Bad Person Illusion.

The Boulder-in-the-Road Illusion

Our differences are irreconcilable;
agreement is impossible.

When we encounter a difference with our boss, spouse or co-worker, and when agreement or cooperation is required to proceed further, an especially disabling misperception arises. It often seems that differences between us are so huge – his character is so devoid of virtue, she is so mean, our values are so opposite – that reconciliation is impossible. A "boulder in the road" blocks any further progress. Faced with the hopelessness of this impasse, we may feel forced to choose between the two Wrong Reflexes – either withdraw from interaction (Distancing), or muster our resources to defeat the Other's resistance (Coercion). Tragically, limiting ourselves to these two ineffective options can lead to escalated hostilities and even divorce, job termination, or pointless legal entanglement.

Why do we perceptually exaggerate the difficulty, to the point of impossibility, of reconciling our differences? Why do we see no way around the boulder in the road? It sometimes seems that the only thing that can be agreed upon is that agreement is impossible.

In fact, there nearly always is a way around the boulder. Rarely are the underlying self-interests of each participant exactly opposite on any issue of genuine importance. Even when self-interests are incompatible, the search for reasonable compromise can find a better path for each participant than continued conflict. My fellow mediators will confirm that the parties in most disputes in which we become involved are initially deeply pessimistic about the likelihood of success. Nevertheless, mediation achieves a both-gain solution in nearly every interpersonal (two-person) conflict.

The Challenge to Interpersonal Peacemaking

So we see how we are, at times, victims of our own instincts. We labor under illusions that one must win and one must lose, that the problem would be solved if only our stubborn Other would admit fault, and, failing these unlikely outcomes, our differences are irreconcilable.

To cope with this awful state of affairs, we see only options: Distancing to keep things smooth, or, when interaction is required, Coercion as a desperate effort to win or at least to avoid losing.

There is an alternative. It is remarkably simple and effective, even though our instinctive blinders often prevent us from seeing it. Using it can produce a surprising transformation that allows reconciliation of differences without withdrawing, without over-powering, and without losing. There is a way around the boulder in the road. Self Mediation helps you and your Other find another route.

An Attitude Shift: *Breakthrough*

When communicating in search of solutions, our initial challenge is to accept the possible existence of a both-gain solution. We need to create a climate where both participants can express a shared interest in resolving the problem in a fair, if yet undiscovered, way. We need a shift in attitudes from "you-against-me" to "us-against-the-problem." In this more trusting climate, fair compromise and mutual concessions can be more safely discussed. Such an attitude shift would truly be a breakthrough.

How can this Breakthrough be achieved? The design of Self Mediation prevents the Wrong Reflexes from occurring, defusing them as "bombs" that destroy dialogue. The attitude shift does not result from persuasion or reasoning, but from psychological forces toward harmony (to be discussed in chapter 19) that are harnessed by the special dialogue occurring in Step 3.

Once this attitude shift occurs, a solution can be found. If a win-win (both-get-everything-we-want) solution exists in the realm of possibilities, it can be mutually sought when we see ourselves as cooperating partners in the search. If only a more modest both-gain outcome is possible, we can more safely make reasonable compromises in the more trusting climate that Self Mediation produces. In either case, a way has been found around the boulder in the road that does not require identifying a loser.

Chapter 5:

THE THREE LEVELS OF CONFLICT

Some conflicts are hardly noticeable as they ebb and flow through our daily social encounters. Others grow into intense disputes that spawn interpersonal tragedies. The severity of conflict ranges from insignificant *Blips* through a middle range of *Clashes* to severe *Crises* that threaten the life of the relationship.

Just as a golfer selects the proper club for the shot, and a mechanic chooses the right tool for the job, different levels of conflict call for different strategies. Self Mediation is designed for conflicts that are more troublesome than passing minor annoyances, but that have not reached crisis proportions. This chapter will describe the level of conflict that this communication tool is designed to resolve – Level 2 Clashes. It will also offer suggestions for dealing constructively with Blips and Crises.

LEVEL 1: *BLIPS*

Blips are inevitable. And some people would find life without Blips boring. For most, few days spent in intensely interdependent interaction with people are entirely free of minor annoyances. But these Blips pose no threat to the relationship, nor do they produce disharmony that breaks down teamwork and blocks satisfaction of needs.

Workplace Example

Jean, a co-worker, has used your coffee cup to water plants in the office. You have asked her to find another water vessel, but this morning she used it again. If you are otherwise cordial and cooperative, this annoyance probably can be handled by reminding Jean of your wishes. A special meeting as called for by Self Mediation is probably unnecessary.

Family Example

Pat, your spouse, occasionally leaves dirty dishes in the sink, despite your request that they be placed in the dishwasher. Usually your request is honored, but this evening you noticed that Pat had left a drinking glass on the counter before going out to exercise. Unless this irritant masks more significant divisive issues in your relationship, another brief mention will probably suffice.

Still, Blips can grow more severe if poorly handled over time. How can we prevent the needless escalation of Level 1 Blips into Level 2 Clashes or Level 3 Crises?

The simplest advice is to routinely refrain from resorting to those outdated Wrong Reflexes – Distancing (Walk-aways) and Coercion (Power-plays) – at *any* time. These behaviors antagonize other people, and, even more importantly, they prevent the communication that is necessary to limit misunderstandings. In other words:

> 1) Do not *ever* walk out, hang up, or otherwise use termination of contact as a retaliatory tactic.

> 2) Do not *ever* use threats, intimidation or coercion to pressure your Other to comply with your wishes.

See Part 6: Common Courtesy for more about these suggestions.

The Gift Exchange

As Blips accumulate and tension mounts, communication breaks down. Before Level 1 Blips become Level 2 Clashes, you can use an intriguing behavioral device to trigger a release of tension in your relationship.

The device consists of initiating an unexpected "gift" – a conciliatory gesture – to the other person. Invite your co-worker to lunch or stop by his office to ask about his children. Give your spouse a warm hug, bring home flowers, or offer to cook dinner. An automatic psychological reflex causes friendly gestures like these to spark a reciprocal gesture – a "gift exchange." If a genuine gift exchange happens, tension can quickly subside and trust may be renewed.

The reflex that prompts your Other to reciprocate your gift is present in everyone. However, certain personality factors can block it from occurring in some people. So, you cannot be sure it will work every time you try it. But your gift costs little, and it can trigger a valuable shift in your relationship from distance to closeness. You accept the risk that your gift will be rejected, that you might be seen as giving in, or as setting a precedent that you do not want to be obligated to in the future. Taking this risk requires courage. Paradoxically, allowing ourselves to appear weak by our vulnerability to rejection requires strength.

What happens if your Other does not return your gift? If your initiatives do not trigger a response after two or three attempts, then it probably will not do so in the future.

A note for business readers: The dynamics of the gift-exchange are psychological and emotional, not rational and logical. The impulse to reciprocate is an unconscious response. In business negotiations, bargaining strategies are often quite conscious. The gift-exchange may not work because skilled negotiators are often trained to divert psychological inducements to make concessions. Although the gift-exchange can be effectively used in business negotiations, be especially careful not to initiate a gift that weakens your bargaining position.

LEVEL 2: *CLASHES*

Self Mediation, the central message of this book, is designed to help us manage differences in good relationships. Clashes happen in good relationships.

Despite our best efforts, Blips sometimes accumulate and grow into Clashes. How do we know when the line has been crossed? Indications are:

- Repeated disputes about the same issue, perhaps spread over days or weeks.
- Arguing over an increasing number of issues.
- Feeling less cooperative toward the Other.
- Feeling less trusting of the Other's sincere good will.

- Remaining angry at the Other for a longer period, perhaps hours or days.
- Beginning to privately question the value of the relationship.
- And, most indicatively, the habitual use of Coercion and/or Distancing tactics in your interactions.

Workplace Example

Your colleague on a project team has made a number of mistakes that you have worked overtime to correct. When confronted, he shrugs it off, dismissing your complaints as unimportant. Your resentment grows as you are unable to get him to acknowledge your needs.

Family Example

You and your spouse have differing styles of handling money. You like to budget carefully and save for special events and vacations. He spends more freely and does not keep track of where money goes. You have had numerous arguments about this, but the pattern continues. Lately, you notice that you both avoid discussing any subject that pertains to family finances.

Part 2 of this book will describe in detail how to use Self Mediation to produce solutions to the issues on which you and your Other clash.

LEVEL 3: *CRISES*

Most of us, at points in life, encounter differences so deep that even regular communication as Self Mediation suggests will not produce satisfaction. Crises call for more help

than this self-help procedure can provide. How can we
distinguish Crises from Clashes? Indications are:

- You have decided to terminate the relationship.
- You fear that your Other will terminate the
  relationship.
- You sense that the relationship is psychologically
  unhealthy, and fear that you are vulnerable to
  emotional harm by remaining in it.
- There is a risk of physical violence.
- Vulnerable people, especially children, are being
  emotionally, physically, or economically hurt by the
  conflict.

Workplace Example

Your boss rated you "unsatisfactory" in your latest
performance appraisal. Believing that the evaluation is unfair,
you have attempted to speak with your boss, only to be told that
it is a closed issue. Your resentment about not being given an
opportunity to rebut the negative appraisal is eroding your
loyalty to your employer.

Option: Request assistance from a qualified
personnel representative or ombudsman who can mediate the
dispute.

Family Example

Despite several discussions using Self Mediation you
and your spouse remain deeply divided on whether to have a
child. You feel you need a child to make your life feel complete,
and your spouse feels that a child would only interfere with

career progress. Whenever the issue is mentioned, you feel deep resentment and despair. You are seriously considering divorce.

Option: See a counselor or family therapist to explore the emotional needs underlying the issue of whether to have children.

What can you do about such severe conflicts? In the most pessimistic analysis, intentionally using the Wrong Reflexes as a coping strategy are options that are still available to you:

Distancing. You may choose to put enough emotional, physical, and functional distance between yourself and your Other to stay safe.

Coercion. You may choose to use threat and manipulation to avoid losing what may be a continuous win-lose conflict.

Of course, neither of these options can bring you satisfaction in the relationship, and with time are likely to lead to further deterioration. Before resigning yourself to such an unhappy fate, consider more constructive solutions:

- Use a neutral mediator (see Part 4: Third-Party Mediation), and/or
- Use a counselor or therapist to gain emotional support and explore how you can best deal with the difficult situation you face.

Crises are dangerous. You may face a painful choice of terminating the relationship or staying in a situation that holds no prospect of satisfaction. Encouragingly, in my work as a professional mediator, I notice that many people judge conflicts as crises when in fact they are resolvable – the Boulder-in-the-

Road Illusion at play with our perceptions. I suggest thinking objectively about your situation, drawing on the information in chapter 15 (When It Works, When It Won't), before deciding how to handle it.

Part 2

SELF MEDIATION

Chapter 6:

A skeleton view of

SELF MEDIATION
A 4-Step Method for Building Better Relationships

The next several chapters will examine in detail each
step of Self Mediation. Before venturing into the trees, let's take
another look at the overview of the forest to get our bearings.

Step 1: **FIND A TIME TO TALK**
The **Approach**
The **Issue Statement**
The **Request**
The **Sale** (if needed)
The **Cardinal Rules** (if needed)
The **Time & Place**

Step 2: **PLAN THE CONTEXT**
Remove the "land mines" from your time-and-place
environment

Step 3: **TALK IT OUT**
The **Opening**
Express appreciation
Express optimism
Reminders: *The Cardinal Rules*
State the issue
The **Invitation**
The **Dialogue**
Task #1: Stay engaged in the *Essential Process*
Task #2: Support *Conciliatory Gestures*
The **Breakthrough**

Step 4: **MAKE A DEAL**
Balanced
Behaviorally specific
Written

Chapter 7:

THE CARDINAL RULES

At the core of Self Mediation are the *Cardinal Rules*, which outlaw the Wrong Reflexes. The effectiveness of this path to interpersonal peace and productivity flows directly from the prohibition of those two self-destructive impulses that destroy relationships. The Cardinal Rules are the interpersonal equivalent of naval "rules of engagement" that assert one's rights while preventing escalation of hostilities.

> #1: ***Do Not Distance.*** Do not use "Walk-aways" to withdraw from communication, whether in self-defense to protect against feeling frustrated and despairing, or in retaliation against the Other.

> #2: ***Do Not Coerce.*** Do not use "Power-plays" to "win" a power struggle by imposing a one-sided solution via threats, ultimatums, intimidation, or other force.

Use these Cardinal Rules during Self Mediation. Indeed, use them as your personal rules of engagement in everyday family and work life. Doing so will produce healthier, more satisfying ongoing interdependent relationships.

In the last chapter of this book you will read about how the spirit of these Cardinal Rules can be applied to everyday living. By renouncing the Wrong Reflexes, and replacing them with "Common Courtesy," it becomes possible to virtually eliminate conflict from your life.

Chapter 8:

Step 1
FIND A TIME TO TALK

Recall that one of our Wrong Reflexes is Distancing. We seek safety by disengaging from the Other, withdrawing, escaping behind a wall of inaccessibility.

Being unavailable for contact ensures that conflict remains unresolved. A sage once said, "Abstinence from communication is the essence of conflict." Without doubt, no resolution is possible without communication. So, the first and most fundamental requirement for resolution is to establish a time in which communication can occur – to have a conversation about having a conversation.

You are fortunate if your Other has read this book and is familiar with Self Mediation – it works even better when both

people know it. But it is likely that on your first attempts, and
on some later occasions, you alone will initiate and actively
manage the process. So let's assume that you are solely
responsible.

The Approach

Get the Other's attention at an appropriate time and
place.

> Example: *"Pat, do you have a minute? Can we talk
> about something?"*

The Issue Statement

Identify the subject that you want to talk about. Take
care to state it in objective terms that do not imply blame or
criticism of the Other. Doing so would unnecessarily arouse
defensiveness and possibly cause your Other to reject your
overture. Also, take care to avoid being drawn into an argument
about the subject at this time. Remember, the purpose of Step 1
is only to "have a conversation about a time to have a
conversation."

> Example: *"We've hit some snags in working together on
> the Atlantic Project. I'm concerned that progress on the
> project is being slowed down because we're not
> communicating well."*

The Request

Ask the Other to join you in having the conversation.

Example: *"I'd like to meet with you at your convenience to talk about this, and to look for ways to improve our teamwork. Are you willing?"*

The Sale (if needed)

Hopefully, your Other will share your concern about the issue and readily agree to meet. But sometimes Others have what sales professionals call "objections" – reasons to reject your proposal. So if objections are raised, you must "sell" your proposal to meet. The basic selling technique is to:
1) Acknowledge the objection
2) Show how acceptance would benefit the other's self-interest
3) Repeat the request.

Example #1: *"I understand that you are busy. It seems that our difficulties have caused each of us to waste unnecessary time. If we could work this out, then we could save time. Do you agree?"*

Example #2: *"I understand your concern that it won't do any good to talk about it. My hunch is that we may not totally understand each other's point of view about this. I'd like to understand yours better. Can we give it a try?"*

Example #3: *"I understand that you feel it is only a minor problem not worth dealing with. How much unnecessary time do you estimate we have spent on this project due to our differences? At our salary levels, that amounts to quite a lot of money. Also, completion of the project has been delayed by a week so far. I'd like to try to avoid additional waste of time. How about it?"*

In this "sales call" you help your Other identify some personal self-interests that are affected by the current conflict, and offer the hope that her interests might be satisfied. It is important that you not convey the impression that this is a manipulative strategy intended to help you and to hurt her. You are making a sincere effort to find a both-gain solution to a shared problem – Self Mediation is *not* self-serving deception. You are merely choosing to act on the assumption that a both-gain solution is possible, and are inviting her to join you in this assumption. Indeed, you may even have troubling doubts, but you are opting for optimism.

Curiously, the Other need not trust that the meeting will be successful or productive, or even believe that any solution is possible other than your acceptance of her previously stated demands. In fact, she is not required to acknowledge that there is a problem at all. You are only asking her to join you in a conversation dedicated to searching for agreement on a particular issue of concern. There is little to lose, and potentially much to gain.

The Cardinal Rules (if needed)

Self Mediation can work only if the dialogue you are arranging is protected from "fatal" violations of the Cardinal Rules. At this point in Step 1, we may need to disarm the Wrong Reflexes by explicitly agreeing to not indulge in those defensive, counterproductive behaviors.

Hopefully, you have no reason to doubt that your Other will be able to stay engaged in conversation long enough to solve the problem without withdrawing (Distancing), and that he can avoid using pressure tactics to impose a one-sided solution (Coercion). However, if your past experience with your Other gives concrete evidence that those risks exist, then you may need to suggest the Cardinal Rules.

> Example: *"I suggest that we both agree to a couple of groundrules.*
>
> *"First, we should not permit any interruptions. So we will not walk out or stop trying before the time has expired that we agree to meet. Also, we should make arrangements to not receive phone calls.*
>
> *"Second, we agree to not use power or force to override the other's objections and impose a one-sided solution. Instead, we try to find a solution that we both can accept.*
>
> *"I accept these groundrules; will you?"*

What about verbal abuse? Inflammatory language, personal insults and name-calling are unpleasant, but are not necessarily fatal Power-plays. You can control your own language, but you have little control over your Other's choice of words. If you feel vulnerable to being verbally abused, you may ask your Other to use restraint. Otherwise, keep in mind the saying, "Sticks and stones may break my bones, but words shall never hurt me."

The Time and Place

Before parting, the practical matter of when and where to meet must be settled. Generally, you, as the initiator of the process, can invite your Other to suggest the setting. Just be mindful of the requirements of Context (discussed in Step 2).

> Example: *"Any private place where we won't be interrupted is fine with me. Where would you like to meet? OK, the third-floor conference room is fine for me, and 3:00 to 4:30 tomorrow is convenient. Good, I'll reserve the room for us. See you then."*

You might consider photocopying Appendix 1 ("Notes for the Other") for your Other to help you Find a Time to Talk. Copyright restrictions are waived for this purpose.

Chapter 9:

Step 2
PLAN THE CONTEXT

The context is the time-and-place environment within which the Dialogue of Step 3 occurs. The purpose of planning the context is to create a setting for effective communication.

Many of our everyday attempts to talk through problems with Others would succeed if it weren't for the distractions and interruptions that unexpectedly arise – "land mines" in the time-and-place terrain that blow up the conversation, sabotaging our efforts. So, Step 2 is simply common-sense prevention of harmful things that might happen in the context of the Dialogue.

This chapter identifies some aspects of context for you to consider. Don't memorize the list. Just know where to turn in this book for quick reference when planning a meeting.

Location

A private place that is free from interruptions should be selected. Importantly, phone calls and people walking in should be prevented. Even music should be eliminated. Moving objects or people are visual distractions. The meeting should occur in a private room that other people will not inadvertently enter. A place where neither person feels on home turf, or a site preferred by your Other, is best.

At the workplace, Dialogues often are held in small conference rooms that can be reserved, or in vacant offices. Your or the Other's office is an alternate choice, if you are certain that interruptions can be prevented.

At home, any comfortable room in the house is OK. It's best if no one else is home at the time, and the phone should be answered by a recording device or left off the hook.

Physical Comforts

Discomforts distract. Soft chairs or couches are better than less comfortable seating. Temperature, lighting, and thirst are possible distractions. Serving or eating food during the meeting is usually not a good idea, but you may want to keep non-alcoholic liquids nearby.

Duration

Note: This section conservatively assumes that you have not used Self Mediation previously with this particular Other, that your Other is not familiar with the method and is somewhat reluctant to participate, and that the conflict is clearly a Clash, not a Blip. If you and your Other habitually abide by the Cardinal Rules during routine communication (congratulations!), then a special lengthy Dialogue may often be unnecessary.

Length of the Dialogue is a crucial factor. It is essential that enough time is available so that the Breakthrough can be reached. If this point of natural closure has not yet occurred when the agreed time period expires, then the meeting may not have helped.

Although some discussions require only a half-hour or less, it is often unwise to begin a Dialogue if you know that you will have to stop so soon. Two hours is usually more than enough. To be safe, you may wish to allot plenty of time.

It is helpful if both people have realistic expectations about the meeting. Each should understand that most of the time in discussion may be spent in frustrating struggle. The Breakthrough and the deal-making that follow take only a short time, but the difficult and often discouraging effort that precedes it is a necessary part of the journey. *You must know this fact and trust its truth, even if your Other does not.*

Quitting the Dialogue before its positive conclusion is the most common cause of failure in using Self Mediation. If you are at all doubtful about the strength of your resolve to stay in stressful confrontation with your Other long enough to reach the Breakthrough (that is, your commitment to Cardinal Rule #1), then I urge you to carefully read Part 5 of this book. The behavioral science explanations for why this persistence pays off may bolster your courage in venturing into a daunting encounter.

Confidentiality

The privacy of things you both say in this meeting should be respected. "Talk-aboutism" – that bad habit of criticizing one person to another – only inflames conflict and undermines success.

At the workplace, the agreement you make may become an announced job activity that is known to colleagues. Also, the fact that the two of you have met to discuss a problem may become common knowledge among co-workers. Still, details of the discussion leading up the deal-making need not be disclosed.

As the initiator of Self Mediation, you have direct control only over your own part in maintaining confidentiality. You can do little to influence your Other's behavior beyond requesting that he afford you the same consideration. If you are unsure about his ability or willingness to do this, you may want to be especially mindful of what you disclose during the Dialogue.

Interruptions

Absolutely none! Make arrangements to have incoming phone calls intercepted by a secretary, or answered by a telephone answering machine. Also, arrange to avoid interruptions by colleagues at work, and by children or friends at home.

Timing

The time of day or time of week can affect energy level, attentiveness, and distractibility during your discussion. The rule of thumb is: Find a time when you both are not too tired or preoccupied with other concerns.

Who Else Is Present?

No one.

Chapter 10:

Step 3
TALK IT OUT

Meeting to talk is the core ingredient of Self Mediation. Steps 1 and 2 are simply preparations for Step 3. Performing your two tasks within the recommended structure and context of the discussion releases energy that is bound up in conflict. That energy can then be applied to cooperative problem-solving, instead of competitive fighting – shifting from "me-against-you" to "us-against-the-problem."

The Structure

The meeting consists of four parts: The *Opening,* the *Invitation,* the *Dialogue,* and the *Breakthrough.* Let's flesh out the skeleton with examples of how each part may be performed.

The OPENING

EXPRESS APPRECIATION
"I appreciate your willingness to meet with me to talk this out."

EXPRESS OPTIMISM
"I'm hopeful that we can find a solution that is beneficial to both of us."

REMINDERS (The Cardinal Rules)

"It's very important that our discussion is not interrupted, and that we don't give up or walk out, even if we get frustrated. Are you certain you can be here until 4:00 if we need to be?

"Also, let's agree for this meeting to refrain from using Power-plays to defeat the other. Instead, let's look for solutions that both might accept. OK?"

STATE THE ISSUE

"My understanding of the issue is that we have different views about what my role is in the Atlantic Project."

The INVITATION

"Please tell me how you see the situation. Help me understand how this affects you."

The DIALOGUE

During the Dialogue, which consumes most of the time in the meeting, you perform two tasks:

Task #1: Ensure that the "Essential Process" continues – permit no Walk-aways and no Power-plays.

Task #2: Support conciliatory gestures* made by the Other, and offer them yourself when you can do so sincerely.

* Conciliatory gestures are defined as "uncoerced behaviors, typically verbal, that display vulnerability to one's adversary." See chapter 19 for a fuller explanation.

Let's take a closer look at how these tasks are performed.

The Essential Process

The "Essential Process" is the form of communication that must happen if we are to reach common ground:

> *Face-to-face talking*
> *about the issues on which we differ*
> *without interruption*
> *for as long as necessary*
> *to reach the "Breakthrough"*

You have initiated Self Mediation and understand its purpose; your Other may not have this understanding. So it is up to you to maintain the process. Common lapses in the Essential Process include:

- Talking about subjects that are not relevant to your relationship (weather, current events, technical information, other safe topics)
- Talking about other people (co-workers, family members) as if they hold the only key to solving your problem
- Telling jokes
- Giving up, expressing hopelessness
- Falling silent

When your Other employs these diversionary tactics, revive the Essential Process with your next comment. Redirect, rather than criticize.

Illustrations:
- *"Let's get back to the problem at hand. How do you feel about . . ."*
- *"I know it seems hopeless, but let's see if we can find a way out of this."*
- *You've been quiet awhile. I'd like to hear about what you are thinking."*

Readiness to let go of one's prior demands results partly from the cathartic effect of talking. Give your Other plenty of opportunity to express opinions, views, feelings, and judgments. Think of your job description during this time as: "To solicit my Other's views on the disputed issue." Listen with as much patience and interest as you can muster.

Of course, much of what your Other says, especially early in the Dialogue, may be difficult for you to hear. She may criticize and blame you, make statements that you feel are unfair or factually incorrect, and repeat old arguments that have angered you in the past. Feeling attacked by these comments may incite you to retaliate. After all, you, too, are only human, and may feel as much resentment toward your Other as she expresses toward you. Like her, you need time to talk and tell your side. You also need to ventilate your pent-up frustrations. If you are confident that your Other will not renege on her commitment to the Cardinal Rules, you can express your anger openly.

Conciliatory Gestures

Conciliatory gestures are the "magic" ingredient in the Self Mediation formula for peace. Initiating and responding constructively to these subtle yet powerful "statements of voluntary vulnerability" is what makes the method work even when our Illusions would have us believe that the situation is irresolvable.

With time (though not as quickly as you might like) you may notice a slackening of the combative "me-against-you" energy that drives your Other's need to oppose you, signaling openness to an "us-against-the-problem" orientation to the problem. Genuine, sincere conciliatory gestures do not occur until aggressive impulses have been somewhat discharged through catharsis and ventilation.

Since you are the one who is managing the Dialogue, it is your job to be alert to the Other's friendly comments. When she expresses a conciliatory gesture, even if you are still angry, try to acknowledge it. And, of course, offer such gestures yourself when you can do so sincerely.

Conciliatory gestures appear in just a few forms, but are infinitely varied within each form. Here is a listing of these types, showing how each one might be expressed and how the Self-mediator might respond. Note that these examples are shown as unambiguous statements. In their natural habitat, conciliatory gestures are typically nested within a self-protective wrapping of criticism or blaming remarks. Consequently, in everyday life, conciliatory gestures often go unnoticed or ignored – opportunities for peacemaking are missed. As the initiator, your task is to listen for, and respond to, these powerful elements of dialogue, seizing upon their promise. A sampling is provided on the next page.

Types of Conciliatory Gestures

Apologizing
  Example: *"I'm sorry that my comments in the staff meeting embarrassed you. It was thoughtless of me."*
  Response: *"I appreciate your apology."*

Owning responsibility
  Example: *"I see now that I have contributed to this problem. I didn't see that before."*
  Response: *"Thanks for recognizing that we both have played a part."*

Conceding
  Example: *"I'm willing to meet with you, if you are willing to do it at a time that is convenient for me."*
  Response: *"Thanks for the offer. When would you like to meet."*

Self-disclosing
  Example: *"I've been worried about what you might do to get back at me, and so I've been avoiding you."*
  Response: *"I appreciate your sharing that with me. I see that this has not been easy for you either."*

Expressing positive feelings for the Other
  Example: *"You are a competent and skilled professional."*
  Response: *"Thanks for the compliment. I recognize your skills too."*

Initiating problem-solving
  Example: *"How do you suggest we solve this?"*
  Response: *"Thanks for asking for my ideas. How about if we . . ."*

Do Not Score Points

Conciliatory gestures always place the person who offers them in a vulnerable position. His Other is presented with an opportunity to take advantage by "scoring a point."

When the Other offers a conciliatory gesture, don't yield to the temptation to score. *Do not take advantage of your Other's vulnerability,* even if he takes advantage of yours. Rejecting the Other's efforts to conciliate is a commonly used retaliatory tactic used during ordinary arguments. But doing so damages trust and widens the gap to be bridged. The Dialogue is not an ordinary argument. For many people, scoring points may be an old bad habit; if it is one of yours, it's time to break it.

The BREAKTHROUGH

Performing these two tasks – staying in the Essential Process, and supporting conciliatory gestures – in this context creates conditions in which voluntary, uncoerced agreement can occur. The Breakthrough happens when you and the Other shift from me-against-you fighting to an us-against-the-problem search for solutions.

On most occasions some agreement, even if limited, can be reached in one Dialogue. If for any reason one meeting does not produce the Breakthrough, *do not give up.* Schedule another time to talk within the next few days, or even better if within a few hours. Don't let this setback squelch your optimism that a way can be found around the boulder in the road.

Often, the passage of a brief period of time after an unsuccessful Dialogue actually allows a face-saving opportunity to make concessions. After a time-break, conciliatory gestures can be justified by "having had a chance to think it over." In reality, "thinking it over" – in the sense of rational analysis – may have had little to do with the shift in attitude. Instead, we are able to have an honorable "change of mind" after a break without appearing to cave in to our Other's pressure. Regardless of motive, the shift will have occurred and agreement reached.

The Spearcatcher Strategy

When using Self Mediation at work, it can be helpful to think of yourself as a "spearcatcher." The spearcatcher realizes that no actual harm can come from "word spears" and so allows them to strike without self-defensive maneuvering. She fearlessly lets verbal slings and arrows hail down upon her, shielded by the knowledge that words can do no physical damage. The spearcatcher actually invites wordspears when she senses the Other is withholding ammunition. Although in battle, she is safe in knowing that absorbing the Other's attack without retaliating is a secret strategy for eliciting a more compromising attitude from the Other.

The spearcatcher stifles her impulse to retaliate. Although she *feels* the impulse to react, she does not *act* on it – she exercises willpower over her own behavior. She presents herself as an available target for the Other's attacks, knowing that his aggressive energy will eventually become spent, leading to his making conciliatory gestures. Then, when the Other is in a more receptive mood, she can negotiate a beneficial agreement.

Illustrations:
- *"How did you feel after I broke my promise?"*
- *"What did you think about me when you found out I was the one who wrote the memo criticizing you?"*

Caution!

Unless both you and your Other are fully knowledgeable about the spearcatcher variation of Self Mediation, I do not advise its use with family members or your closest work associates.

Why? In relationships with spouses, siblings and children, we want emotional intimacy. This is also often true of business partners and close teammates, though typically to a lesser extent. In contrast, our goal in relation to many co-workers, bosses, subordinates and other work associates is often simply to be able to work together cooperatively in performing our jobs – emotional intimacy is not sought.

By its nature, spearcatching is a deceptive maneuver. It speeds up the emergence of conciliatory gestures from your Other, but misleads him to believe that your receptiveness and apparent openness to his arguments are genuine. In truth, your acquiescence is not entirely sincere. It is unlikely that you will have been convinced by your Other's argument that he is right and that you are wrong. By neglecting to defend yourself, you are allowing him to make a false assumption. You are permitting him to think that you have conceded some points; but your real intent is to shape his emotional state into a less defensive form that will more likely lead to concessions on the issues that are of real interest to you. Using spearcatching

regularly as a covert strategy with family members can erode
trust and promote dishonest relationships.

A Better Way

By staying in problem-focused conversation, we act *as if*
there were a both-gain solution, rather than allowing the Win-
Lose Illusion to control us. Assuming that only win-lose
outcomes are possible leads to Distancing and Coercion
strategies – Walk-aways and Power-plays. The both-gain
assumption permits a mutually satisfactory solution to be found
whenever possible; assuming it is a win-or-lose situation
precludes this possibility.

So we recognize that there is an alternative to the Wrong
Reflexes that all too often keep conflicts unresolved. The
alternative is *staying in process* – specifically, the Essential
Process. The passage of time in uninterrupted communication
eventually permits the forces harnessed by Self Mediation to
bring harmony to discordant relationships.

Chapter 11:

SKILLS FOR DIALOGUE

Self Mediation overcomes the most prevalent obstacles to interpersonal peace: The Wrong Reflexes. Simply engaging in face-to-face conversation in the appropriate context while complying with the Cardinal Rules helps people manage their differences and build more satisfying relationships.

But the skeptical reader is asking, "What about skills? Aren't special skills needed in the Dialogue?"

How old are you? You have that number of years' experience studying at the University of Life. You have learned more than you may realize about how to communicate, about how to get along with others. Of course, we also learn ineffective communication patterns along with more positive skills. But, on balance, most adults who are able to maintain friendships, hold jobs, join groups, and survive the crucible of family life possess sufficient communication skills to make Self Mediation work.

Still, let's not ignore the contributions of the applied behavioral sciences that can enhance our ability to use Self

Mediation successfully. Three social skills are especially helpful: *Listening, Negotiation,* and *Assertiveness.*

LISTENING

If talking and listening are the two acts of oral communication, listening is the nobler half.

Listening demonstrates openness to what the Other is saying. How can this receptivity be conveyed during the Dialogue? Here are some specific listening tools:
- Keeping steady eye contact
- Not interrupting
- Not giving advice
- Summarizing what you have heard
- Making reflective statements, showing that you understand how the Other feels

Hostile enemies don't listen. Using these listening tools demonstrates to the Other that you are not a hostile enemy, and that you are open to considering his needs and concerns. Sensing that his needs are respected, your Other will be less compelled to escalate aggression to prevail in persuading you to accept his views. By listening, you are demonstrating that you are not hiding behind the impenetrable shield of sealed ears, but are open and receptive to the Other. You are willing to hear.

NEGOTIATION

We get our needs met by others through negotiation. Some popular writers have equated negotiation with "power bargaining" in which the needs of the Other are not considered. But here we are concerned with managing differences in ongoing interdependent relationships. Our needs are mutual and reciprocal. Power bargaining erodes trust and goodwill. So such a strategy is short-sighted at best, and self-destructive at worst.

A better model for the Dialogue is "principled negotiation"* which consists of four basic guidelines for interaction. To the extent that we can behave according to these principles during the Dialogue, the more effective Self Mediation will be in producing agreement.

1) Separate the PERSON from the PROBLEM.

Certain characteristics of your Other may annoy you. Her values may offend you. His lack of social grace may irritate you. As much as you might wish these characteristics to change, they will not. Your Other will remain the same person with much the same psychological make-up, despite   your rehabilitative efforts on his behalf. Furthermore, criticizing personal characteristics will only inflame the conflict by arousing defenses. So how can the situation change? Happily, the conflict can be resolved without changing the person. Do your best to avoid discussing personal characteristics, either your own or your Other's. Focus instead on the problem – the issues on which agreement or joint action is sought.

*Adapted from Roger Fisher and William Ury, *Getting to Yes*. Boston: Houghton Mifflin, 1981.

2) <u>Focus on INTERESTS, not POSITIONS.</u>

Conflicts happen in part because disputants hold (apparently) incompatible positions on one or more issues. As songwriter Paul Simon melodiously remarked, "You want to sleep with the window open, I want to sleep with the window closed, good-bye, good-bye, good-bye." Here the issue in contention is whether the window should be open or closed while the couple sleeps. The diametrically opposed positions that the two bedmates hold have apparently led to dissolution of their relationship – an interpersonal tragedy.

The trap of debating *positions* is that the best possible solution is a splitting-the-difference compromise. The essence of compromise is that neither disputant gets what she wants. Position-based bargaining is a win-lose power struggle.

But every position put forth by disputants rests on underlying *self-interests,* which may be unclear even to oneself. If instead of arguing about positions we probe for our own and the other's underlying self-interests, then both-gain alternatives may come into view. "How does sleeping with the window closed affect me?" "What do you like about sleeping with the window open?" By exploring the answers to such questions, it becomes conceivable that both disputants' self-interests may be satisfied, and that neither must lose.

3) <u>Invent OPTIONS for mutual gain</u>.

Interest-based bargaining promotes a less contentious climate in the Dialogue, which aids the search for both-gain solutions. In this more collaborative mode, together you may search creatively for alternatives that might benefit both of you. Now the Dialogue is a problem-solving discussion where your orientation is us-against-the-problem rather than me-against-you.

Ideally, both disputants can brainstorm possible solutions, listing as many ideas as you can think of without worrying about how practical or promising they are. Once a pool of alternative solutions has been brainstormed, each option can be tested for compatibility with each disputant's underlying self-interests.

4) Identify objective CRITERIA.

To agree on an issue is to make a joint decision. Decisions are always based on criteria for judging whether they are good or bad decisions.

In typical arguments (searches for a joint decision), these criteria are generally not conscious or explicit. But just because we are not aware of them doesn't mean decision criteria are not present. Let's say you have decided to go to Tony's Pizzaria for dinner tonight rather than Wong's Rice Kitchen. How did you make that decision? If you answer, "Because I like the food better" or "Because I like the atmosphere better," then we now know that the criterion for the decision about where to eat tonight was "The food must be good" or "The atmosphere must be pleasant." That is, a good decision must meet these criteria. A bad decision would fail to meet these criteria.

An objective criterion is neutral with respect to the self-interests of the disputants. That is, an unbiased observer would say that your agreement is a fair one. If the criteria for agreement between you and your Other are objective, rather than subjective, then your agreement is more stable and likely to last. If criteria are subjective, then one disputant will feel that the decision was unfair and therefore will not feel motivated to implement it.

Return to our conflict over sleeping with the window open or closed. An objective criterion for deciding what to do about the problem might be: "Both people have the right to sleep comfortably." Therefore, a fair solution will permit each person to sleep comfortably. An agreement (joint decision) that satisfies that criterion will be a good one.

ASSERTIVENESS

If I could grant my children only one social skill, it would be assertiveness.

Let's define what we mean by this often misunderstood idea. It is best understood as one of three social behaviors taken together:

Aggression: Behavior that violates another person's rights.

Submission: Behavior that allows another person to violate one's rights.

Assertion: Behavior that insists on one's rights without violating the rights of others.

Readers who are familiar with East-Asian cultures will recognize that, at least in hierarchical organizations, submission to superiors is necessary to survival. To behave assertively risks causing loss of face to the superior, and promptly leads to social ostracism of the assertive person. Within a Western cultural context, however, I assert the following two value judgments:

- Assertiveness is *good* difference-managing behavior.
- Aggressiveness and submissiveness are *poor* difference-managing behaviors.

Aggressiveness sparks defensiveness in others. Also, aggressiveness is its behavioral expression – the way we act when we feel defensive. Submissiveness may be a useful short-term strategy to avoid confrontation, but it sows the seeds for resentments that flower into future episodes of conflict.

Again illustrating with the open/closed window conflict, the bedmate who slams down the window and shouts threateningly at the Other to leave it down is behaving aggressively. The Other's rights to have his comfort considered have been violated. If the bedmate who was shouted at gives up the struggle and sleeps poorly because of the stuffy air, he is behaving submissively. This bedmate, having his rights violated, will surely feel resentful. This state of affairs does not promote interpersonal peace.

An alternative to submissiveness is assertiveness: "I want to sleep comfortably – cooling ventilation would help me do that." By stating one's needs and insisting that they be considered by the bedmate, one is more likely to find a mutually acceptable solution to the issue. Even if a both-gain solution is not found, one can more willingly accept a less-than-ideal solution without holding a residue of hostility, ready to burst out in response to the next triggering event.

Bumpy, But a Road Nonetheless

So listening, asserting your needs, and negotiating on principle in the Dialogue will help you reach the Breakthrough. Even if your skills in these areas are lofty, you will find the road bumpy. There exists no smooth avenue to interpersonal peace. Those of us with more yet to learn must abide the ruts and potholes. Just do your best with the skills you have gained in the school of life. The road may be rough, but it leads to a destination worth reaching.

Chapter 12:

Step 4
MAKE A DEAL

For many people, the most surprising part of Self Mediation is the Breakthrough, the shift in attitude from me-against-you to us-against-the-problem. Defensiveness, mistrust, and vengefulness lift like morning fog from the interpersonal battlefield, revealing possible routes around the Boulder in the Road. Both you and your Other are now emotionally ready to join efforts in mutually searching for the best route.

Why does the Breakthrough happen? Ironically, it does not ensue from logical persuasion, rational thinking, or reasonable problem-solving, although we may think so at the time. Instead, it springs automatically from several psychological forces that converge to produce this naturally occurring event. Chapter 19 will discuss these forces.

The Breakthrough opens a window of opportunity in which both participants are willing to agree about something. Together, you can take advantage of this mutual openness to agree about something of importance to each of you. More than producing goodwill, a Deal prescribes how you will interact with one another in the future. The most successful agreements are *balanced, behaviorally specific,* and *written.*

BALANCED

Often, a Deal consists of an exchange of concessions from each person – "I'll do this if you'll do that" – that allows both people to gain. On occasion, a creative solution is found that satisfies each participant's needs while requiring no concessions from either – the rare "win-win" outcome.

Whether a dramatic discovery of similar underlying self-interests, or simply a fair compromise involving concessions, the Deal should be balanced. That is, each person should gain a personal benefit from the Deal. Their gains need not be exactly equal, but the Deal should give each person an incentive for doing her part in the future. An unbalanced agreement is a short-lived agreement.

BEHAVIORALLY SPECIFIC

The Deal captures in specific behavior the spirit of goodwill present at the Breakthrough.

Agreements that are too general or that concern our thoughts, attitudes or values can fail because we can't see or hear thoughts, attitudes and values. These "mental events" are invisible, hidden inside our heads. Agreements about behaviors that can be seen or heard are verifiable.

For example, your agreement to "respect my wishes" or "be open and honest" may unravel because we cannot verify whether you are in fact "respecting my wishes" or "being honest." You may claim that you are; I may feel that you are not.   Intentions are not as easy to discern as behaviors.

So we should frame agreements that are specific as to *who* is to do *what,* by *when,* for *how long,* under what *conditions.*   If a Deal is behaviorally specific, it will be easy to determine how fully each person has lived up to it.

During the Deal-making part of the Dialogue, it is helpful to test proposed parts of the agreement for behavioral specificity. Useful questions to ask:
- *"How will I be able to tell that you are* [respecting my wishes]?"
- *"What behaviors will I see and hear if you are* [being open and honest]?"

The result will be a clear mutual understanding of how the Deal will be carried out. If you are deciding which of you is to make the sales trip to Kansas City, all compromises and concessions are detailed. If you are defining responsibilities in the Atlantic project, all aspects of your interdependent roles will be described. This clarity results in a separation of *your* responsibilities from *my* responsibilities in solving *our* problem.

WRITTEN

Normally, agreements are more complicated than simple yes-or-no decisions or other easy-to-remember solutions. Recording Deals in mutually acceptable terms will help protect against selective memory loss in the future. Each person should keep copies of the written document. Sometimes questions arise in the future about what was actually agreed to. The written document is objective evidence that can help answer such questions.

Personal Responsibility

No Deal will work unless each person accepts individual responsibility for doing her part. The universal obstacle we confront when struggling with differences is how to separate *my* responsibilities from *yours* in solving *our* problem. Using Self Mediation solves that dilemma – a behaviorally specific agreement separates each person's responsibilities from the other's.

Once the agreement is described in behavioral detail, it is then up to each partner to fulfill the responsibility that is uniquely and clearly hers – a much easier challenge. Once a

Deal has been created that serves each partner's self-interests, both people have an incentive to responsibly perform her part.

Limiting the Duration of the Deal

It may be helpful to agree in advance to limit the length of time that the agreement will be in force. That is, you may prefer to commit to it for only one week or one month. Then you can plan to renegotiate parts of the agreement. Until that time, you should obligate yourself to doing what you have agreed to do, even if it begins to feel unfair or unsatisfactory after a while.

Is a Deal Always Necessary?

Much of the Dialogue's value is simply in opening lines of communication. Although words can hurt, face-to-face communication is also a healing and restorative medicine for wounded relationships. So, the particular items of agreement may be of only secondary importance.

This is especially true of managing differences between marital partners. In fact, Step 4 may be ignored entirely when there is no problem to solve – just "talk it out" occasionally to renew trust and affection.

Often, however, a decision about a joint course of action must be made and implemented, such as choosing which new automobile to buy, or selecting the salesperson to make that trip to Kansas City next week. Typically, workplace conflicts involve business problems that call for solution. In these instances, whether at work or home, the Breakthrough presents an important opportunity to make a Deal about a problem that requires an answer.

The Bottom Line

The question of whether making a Deal is necessary reduces to this:

- If a decision or course of action related to the contested issue requires the consent or involvement of both persons, then a Deal must be made.
- If not, concluding the Dialogue with an agreement is optional. Still, doing so may help participants feel a satisfying sense of closure.

SAMPLE AGREEMENT

Issue: How Angela and Sean can handle evening household chores.

Angela agrees to not make any requests or demands of Sean for one half hour after he comes home from work. After that time has elapsed, she may ask him to help her prepare dinner and help with the kids. She agrees not to scold or criticize him for whatever he may choose to do during his "sacred half hour."

Benefit for Angela: She gains Sean's voluntary help during suppertime and with the children.

Sean agrees that after his "sacred half hour" has passed, he will participate with Angela in doing jobs around the house until dinner is over, the dishes are done, and the kids are in bed. He agrees to do the tasks that she asks him to do in meal preparation, clean-up, and getting the kids ready for bed. During his half hour, he may rest, read, work at his desk, or whatever else he chooses. Sean agrees that it is his responsibility to tell Angela when his half hour is up and that he is ready to join her. He understands that if he does not announce the end of his time within 30 minutes of its start, then Angela has the right to ask him to begin helping.

Sean agrees that his half-hour is over no later than 6:00, even if he gets home after 5:30 – no excuses for being late.

Benefit for Sean: He gets to unwind in peace after work.

We agree to implement this agreement every workday from now until we talk again in three weeks.

Use It or Lose It

This completes our description of Self Mediation for managing differences at work and home. Try it. Do the best you can. Don't be reluctant to use it because you fear you don't understand it well enough. The method is robust – it tolerates mistakes and imperfections. Just keep in mind the most vital ingredient, the Essential Process:

Face-to-face talking
about the issues on which we differ
without interruption
for as long as necessary
to reach the Breakthrough

In the Dialogue, act how you *choose* to act, not how you *feel* like acting. Choice requires *courage* more than skill.

Practice using it. After one or two successes, your guidance for future uses of Self Mediation will come from your own experience as a self-mediator – not from the words in this book.

Part 3

LIMITATIONS

Chapter 13:

RESOLUTION IS NONRATIONAL

*The problem does not have to be solved
for the conflict to be resolved.*

"Balderdash!" you exclaim. "That doesn't make sense!"
Let's take a closer look.

Many people find it surprising that the path to harmony
often winds through a jungle where anger, resentment and
similar "negative" feelings flourish. You have noticed that Self
Mediation does not discourage the expression of these feelings –
indeed, it actually permits their ventilation, seeming to contradict
popular admonitions to "put on a happy face" and "be logical."

A Lesson from Psychology

One of the common tasks of psychotherapists is to help
clients become aware of their repressed anger, helping them
learn to express it in nondestructive, nonviolent, healthy ways.
Seldom do therapists find it fitting to help their clients suppress

angry feelings. We know that repressed anger is a primary cause of neurosis, particularly depression, and that it poisons interpersonal relationships.

The "Talk It Out" step of Self Mediation provides a structured, safe opportunity for the constructive expression of anger. This is necessary. We must go through, not around. Finding interpersonal harmony requires contact without Coercion, dialogue without Distancing.

To be clear, anger need not be acted out as a high-decibel verbal assault. Anger can also be expressed as firm, assertive declarations of one's needs, interests, and perceptions. Many of us prefer the latter, but some people are more accustomed to the former. Although acting out anger with verbal aggression makes Self Mediation a blunt and bruising instrument, the operation can nevertheless be a success.

Reason and Emotion

Conflict is not resolved by reason alone. In fact, reasonableness has little to do with it, notwithstanding cherished beliefs about human rationality. Intellectual elitists may sneer at the proposition that our beliefs and attitudes are not entirely the result of "logical analysis of the facts."

A discussion of "substantive" and "emotional" issues, which exist in all conflicts, awaits you in chapter 18. For now, we'll just point out that Self Mediation produces both substantive and emotional outcomes:

> 1) Substantive: A mutually acceptable solution to the disputed issue that satisfies both parties' *objective* self-interests.
>
> 2) Emotional: Enhancement of mutual trust, respect, acceptance, and intimacy -- how we *feel* in the relationship.

The resolution of emotional issues affects our *subjective* experience of the relationship, which is not directly determined by the *objective* facts. No doubt you've observed one person being angry and upset about a situation that is sanguinely accepted by another.

How can this be? If we both see the same facts, why don't we have the same experience?

We are propelled into conflict by the appearance of incompatible positions on a substantive issue – I want "A" whereas you want "B." But what *appear* as substantive issues that we believe represent our differences in rational (objective) self-interests are often, in reality, mere façades concealing perceived threats to our underlying emotional needs. That is, those issues are mostly "pseudo-substantive" – a term to be further developed in chapter 18.

So, what we consciously *think* we are doing during dialogue is solving a substantive problem, when in fact we are actually – and not so consciously – seeking resolution of our emotional needs.

Interdependency

When we are not very interdependent – that is, when our emotional needs for each other are of low intensity – our differences can be managed handily. We can be generous and flexible, compromising on substantive issues because not much is at stake for us emotionally.

In contrast, conflicts that occur in our most important relationships, at work and in our families, concern us more deeply. Our needs for trust, intimacy, and cooperation are at stake. These are deeply emotional, not rational. Is distrust amenable to rational solution? How about fear? Or hurt? Clearly, resolution of such needs is not as easy as compromising on a budgetary matter. Trust-building takes time. Specifically, it takes time in dialogue, time in contact, time together that is uncontaminated by Walk-aways and Power-plays – time in the Essential Process.

So, when we use Self Mediation in our most intensely interdependent relationships, the solution to substantive issues is secondary to the resolution of emotional issues. That is, the objective facts in dispute are less important than our subjective experience of being in the relationship.

Consequently, it may be necessary to have many conversations about a substantive issue before it is solved, all the while keeping the conflict resolved by minimizing perceived threats to our emotional issues. We may engage in recurring dialogues with our business partner about a major strategy decision, such as whether to add a new line of products. Or we may talk often and long with our spouse about a deeply important substantive issue like where to live, whose career takes precedence, or whether to have a child. Such momentous decisions could not, and should not, be made in one sitting.

Still, by spending a lot of time in the Essential Process, over weeks or months, we resolve emotional issues. Anxiety is the natural and automatic response to prolonged uncertainty about how our emotional needs will be met. But uncertainty is inevitable as we dialogue about the complex substantive issues. Time-in-dialogue resolves the recurring conflicts while we solve the substantive problem.

Therefore, using Self Mediation repeatedly in our most interdependent relationships builds and maintains a climate of trust, acceptance, and cooperation. In this climate, the weighty substantive issues can eventually be solved, with a maximum of rationality and reason. The idea of applying the principles of Self Mediation in everyday life is developed further in chapter 21, which introduces the concept of "Common Courtesy."

No Quick Fix

We see, then, that a single dose of Self Mediation cannot heal a broken relationship – at least not a deeply interdependent one. The positive effects on trust and cooperativeness that are produced by each Dialogue are reinforced and supported by successive Dialogues. Those who pine for quick fixes may be disappointed by this harsh fact. But those who desire to build good relationships at work and home, and are willing to expend some effort, will be encouraged that there really is a light at the end of the tunnel – it's not a train coming our way, as we may often fear.

So the simplistic notion that we solve our conflicts by reason alone is tossed on the trash heap of our naiveté. Rather, we must entrust ourselves to a process over which we cannot have sole or direct control, and which may not even make rational sense to us. Paradoxically, accepting that we cannot force the outcome we want, we must trust the process to bring it to us: "Let it go, and it will come to you."

On Tolerating Discomfort

Perhaps someone with the self-discipline of a Zen master is able to become emotionally detached enough to not feel uncomfortable during Dialogue. The rest of us mortals don't have such control over our emotions; we find conflict unpleasant. Self Mediation requires that we deal with the Other face-to-face, tolerating a tense, charged atmosphere while talking it out. This communication tool is conceptually simple and behaviorally doable, but not so emotionally easy. Using it calls on us to accept temporary discomfort. We must make a conscious decision in advance to withstand momentary disquiet in order to attain our wish of a better relationship.

With practice, the knowledge that you are acting choicefully and purposefully, accompanied by your growing confidence that Self Mediation actually works, will diminish the discomfort you feel. Still, until we join the Zen masters in the monastery, Dialogues will be stressful. Using this peacemaking procedure requires strength in tolerating discomfort, not weakness in avoiding it.

Chapter 14:

WHAT IT CAN DO, WHAT IT CAN'T

In my practice of mediation with organizations and families, I encounter a frequently held wish – people want a magic wand to banish conflict.

Our desire for peace is surely understandable, but it can lead to trouble. If unchecked, the hope for conflict to disappear brings the expectation that if mediation is successful, my clients' relationship will be free of conflict in the future. If that is my mission, I am doomed to failure.

A Fantasy

Our fantasy is that conflict should be absent in "good" relationships. We regard conflict as a social disease, and assume that there must be a cure.

We seem to relish this idealistic fantasy, and suffer disappointment repeatedly as the plague of conflict infects our relationships. We seem unable to grasp the fact that conflict is as inherent to relationships as "wet" is to water. When pressed, we may grudgingly acknowledge that conflict is part of the package we buy when we join with others in interdependency. But an interlude of peace causes the fantasy to rise again like a phoenix from the ashes of interpersonal war. Beware of its return. Take note:

Self Mediation cannot cure conflict.

Clinging to the impossible dream of a conflict-free relationship with your spouse, boss, child, co-worker, roommate, or sibling may jeopardize your ability to use Self Mediation effectively. Holding up that fantasy as a gauge for measuring success, you will always be disappointed. You might reject whatever gains you achieve because they don't match your expectations. Do not repeat the folly of the hungry fisherman who throws back a small catch in disgust because it would not fill his skillet. Take nourishment even from small portions and imperfect successes.

So the question for this chapter is not, "Why is conflict inevitable?" Let us accept that truism as an unwelcome fact of life. Rather, let's consider the question, "What can I realistically expect to gain by using Self Mediation?"

Again: Relationships and Needs

Let's revisit the metaphor introduced in chapter 1 that views relationships as vehicles for the satisfaction of partners' needs. Each of us has needs that we look to the Other to satisfy; our relationship is the vehicle that transports that satisfaction. The more the vehicle must carry, the greater the weight of its load. Sometimes, the weight exceeds the vehicle's capacity.

Even strong relationships have limits. When the vehicle is overburdened, some needs don't get met. Further, they are weakened when time for communication is insufficient. Spouses who have their own careers, colleagues who are busy with their own jobs, bosses who have other obligations than supporting our work, adult siblings who have their own family responsibilities – these other activities squeeze out the time and energy available for communication between partners. They are loads that weigh down the vehicle of our relationship so that little capacity is left for attending to our needs. When the vehicle is loaded to its limit, we have nothing left to give.

When partners' needs of the Other overload the vehicle's ability to carry them, some needs remain unmet. Consequently, one may feel undernourished in the relationship. It is a short step from feeling undernourished to feeling resentful toward the other for depriving us of needed nourishment. That step requires only an event, remark or circumstance that is *perceived* to mean that the Other is unconcerned about me, hostile toward me, annoyed with me. Note the emphasis is on *perception*. The actual intent is irrelevant. We behave and respond according to how we interpret others' behavior, not to its actual meaning.

Selective Perception

Once mistrust of the Other's motives and feelings toward us begins, additional evidence gathers to corroborate our perception. Information accumulates to support pre-existing perceptions because of the distorting effect of "selective perception."

We need the world around us to make sense – we need consistency. If new information doesn't fit with what we already think we know, we distort the incoming information to make it consistent with the old. So new information passes through a perceptual filter that screens out inconsistencies.

How does selective perception lead to interpersonal conflict? Because of our need for internal consistency, we distort our perceptions of interactions with others so that we selectively let in information that tells us "I am right." Information that tells us "I am wrong" does not pass so easily through our perceptual filters. So, bit by bit, data gather to form a convincing case that confirms our suspicions about the Other's feelings and attitudes about us.

Reality-testing

Unless our internal perceptions are tested against external reality (what the Other *really* means), inaccuracies can grow. Talking together tests the accuracy of our perceptions against the replies of our partner. Effective day-to-day management of interpersonal differences requires conversation.

When interdependency is high and time for communication is limited, the burden on both persons' abilities to efficiently check out perceptions is heavy. Being busy people, time is seldom so abundant that the burden of reality-testing does not occasionally exceed our abilities to communicate, to hear and understand the Other.

The challenge posed by selective perception is daunting enough. To make matters worse, we are simultaneously handicapped by our two Wrong Reflexes – Distancing and Coercion. These communication straight-jackets even further

diminish our ability to stay in face-to-face contact long enough
to complete the task of reaching an agreement.

Realistic Expectations

So it is that we face this stark situation in our everyday
workplace and family relationships. How does Self Mediation
help us? In the Dialogue, we:
- nullify the Wrong Reflexes by adopting the Cardinal
  Rules.
- require sustained face-to-face discussion in the
  Essential Process, and
- harness the power of several psychological forces
  toward harmony (to be discussed in chapter 19).

As a result, we can expect:
- to hear that the Other values our relationship, as do we
  (though not always to an equal degree),
- to learn about demands on the Other that prevent her
  being able to satisfy our needs,
- to discover that some of our assumptions and
  perceptions about what he has been thinking and
  feeling are incorrect, and
- to increase our mutual willingness to compromise in
  order to maintain the relationship.

But even these four modest outcomes cannot be viewed
as permanent gains that can never be lost. Our struggle is like
that of the frog attempting to escape from a well. He hops three
inches, only to slide back two.

Relationships are not static. They are dynamic, living
things that are buffeted daily by new events carried on the
unrelenting tide of time. The improved mutual understanding

and clarified perceptions resulting from Dialogue are covered by the sediment of each day's new events.

Maintenance

Interpersonal relationships need maintenance, just as machinery needs maintenance. Without regular attention to critical points in the system, deterioration in performance will result.

If a relationship has been painfully strained for a long time, one dose of this simple medicine may feel like dramatic progress. Its effects may last for days, weeks or longer. For a more regularly maintained relationship, however, one dose may not have such dramatic effects, because peace is not in such short supply.

How do we maintain relationships? In productive, satisfying pairs, the Cardinal Rules are habitual, regular, even automatic. Partners talk to each other frequently. They do not resort to using the Wrong Reflexes, even under stress. They don't walk out on each other during arguments. They remain physically and emotionally accessible to the other while anger is expressed. They do not use coercion or intimidation to force the other to comply with their demands. Their decisions are made by mutual consent, not by overriding the Other's objections. And they acknowledge the Other's conciliatory gestures so that vulnerability, trust, and openness are rewarded rather than punished. These practices are as important for maintaining good workplace relationships as they are for good marriages.

In other words, partners practice "Common Courtesy" (to be developed in chapter 21).

What Is a "Good" Relationship?

But, differences can erupt into episodes of conflict in even the best of relationships. Because partners experience needs that they properly expect the Other to satisfy, they are interdependent. Their needs, even when occasionally satisfied, do not disappear, just as hunger for food does not vanish forever just because you enjoy a satisfying meal.

So, the difference between a "good" relationship and a "bad" one is not the presence or absence of conflict. The difference lies in the process by which conflicts are resolved. If the process is characterized by the communication principles discussed here, it is good. If the process is characterized by the Wrong Reflexes in their myriad forms, it is bad. Good relationships are satisfying and make us happy. Bad relationships are frustrating and make us unhappy. Knowing how to use Self Mediation empowers us by giving us a choice – we are no longer helpless victims of Others' choices. Which do you prefer?

Chapter 15:

WHEN IT WORKS, WHEN IT WON'T

I herald bad news and good news. Bad news: Self Mediation does not work every time. Good news: After you read this chapter, you will know when it works and when it won't.

The Clashes arising from differences in most relationships can be managed satisfactorily by this method. Some conflicts, however, lack certain requirements that are necessary for success. This chapter describes the eight prerequisites to confidence that Self Mediation will work.

Personality Factors

When involved in "personality clashes," we often conclude that the conflict is irresolvable due to the Other's personality – the Bad Person Illusion. In truth, certain personality factors can indeed impinge on the method, making it less effective. So, some relevant personality factors will be mentioned as we list the eight prerequisites.

Self Mediation is designed for use when all of the following are true:

Prerequisite #1:

It Is a Two-Person Conflict

Some of the components of Self Mediation are used in team building, family consultation, intergroup problem-solving, and labor contract negotiations, to name a few occasions where conflicts need resolution. However, when there are several conflicting parties, or when a party to the conflict consists of more than one person, a more complex resolution strategy is usually necessary.

Often, a conflict that appears to involve several people can be redefined so that it can be at least partially resolved by just two people. Let's say your work team is experiencing a lot of conflict, yet the team leader is doing nothing about it. You can approach a key teammate and use Self Mediation to resolve some problems between the two of you, despite the ongoing conflict on the entire team.

Prerequisite #2:

The Two People Have an
Ongoing, Interdependent Relationship

The participants must be in an important relationship that is not expected to end in the near future. You may be annoyed by the rudeness of a bank teller or the impatience of a telephone operator, but these relationships are not ongoing. Nor do you and he depend on each other for satisfaction of needs, except in very limited or infrequent transactions.

Self Mediation is normally inappropriate and unnecessary when a relationship exists only for the negotiation of one or a few issues, such as the purchase price of an item.

When there is no need to interact, there is no problem. Examples: A divorced couple with no children, and employees whose jobs do not require that they work together. The individuals may not like each other, but their conflicts can best be managed by avoiding contact. Here, there is little consequence to using Wrong Reflex #1: Distancing. Dislike between people who have no needs that the other must satisfy is not an interpersonal conflict.

If a specific situation has come to mind while reading this section that you wish were resolved, but that does not seem to meet this prerequisite, then I suspect you are in fact interdependent. The needs you have of the Other may just be undefined.

Prerequisite #3:

Both People Are Present and Involved in the Dialogue

It takes two hands to clap. An interpersonal conflict is a dyadic, or two-person, process. One person can solve a personal problem; it takes two to solve an interpersonal problem. Unless both parts of the dyad are involved, the problem cannot be solved – the clapping makes no sound. The amount of interest each of you has in resolving the conflict may be unequal, and your levels of enthusiasm for talking about it may differ. If you question your Other's willingness to be involved, review the minimum requirements of your partner as

discussed in chapter 8. Surprisingly little commitment is
expected of her to make Self Mediation work.

Personality factor: *Schizoid Compromise*

Some people's experience in early childhood taught them
that relationships are dangerous. They learned that being
vulnerable to others carries a high risk of being hurt. Trusting
brought abuse. Wanting love brought rejection.

The hurt that relationships can cause children is of two
types: *Invasion* (being emotionally suffocated, humiliated,
battered) and *abandonment* (being left needy, unloved without
emotional contact with others). Adults who suffered as children
in these ways unconsciously stay emotionally distant from others
as a protection against more hurt.

Of course, all of us keep a certain distance, fearing
vulnerability, yet needing interpersonal contact. By the time we
reach adulthood, we have usually found a comfortable
compromise between emotional contact and distance in our
relationships. In psychotherapy, this comfort level is called the
"schizoid compromise."

Due to having suffered traumatic invasion or
abandonment as children, some people are unable to tolerate the
anxiety aroused by sustained face-to-face contact with their
Other, as required in the Dialogue. Being confronted with the
Other's anger, and having the comfortingly familiar Wrong
Reflexes outlawed by the Cardinal Rules, can arouse intolerable
fears. The primitive anxiety of being invaded and destroyed by
the Other's anger, or of being abandoned and losing the
relationship, can be too much to bear. Although Dialogues can
be tense encounters for anyone, some people find it impossible
to remain engaged in uninterrupted issue-focused conversation.

The more emotionally distant is one's schizoid compromise, the less able is the person to stay in the Essential Process, and therefore the effectiveness of Self Mediation is diminished.

The schizoid compromise doesn't influence only intimate and family relationships. This anxiety-regulating mechanism controls our behavior during conflicts in the workplace just as it does in marriages.

Prerequisite #4:

Each Person Is Able to Refrain from Physical Violence

The Dialogue calls for participants to join in verbal, not physical, confrontation. Verbal aggression is permissible, in lieu of more healthy assertiveness, as discussed early in the chapter on skills for dialogue. Physical aggression, however, is clearly impermissible. Not only is violent assault destructive to relationships, it is also illegal. Each person must be able to participate in discussion without fear that the Other's anger may erupt in physical attack.

Personality factor: *Impulsivity*

Most personality traits are present to some degree in all of us. "Impulsivity" is one such trait – the degree to which we have difficulty refraining from acting on our impulses. If your Other has a history of impulsive violence, she may be unable to tolerate the stress of the Dialogue without violent outburst. You may not wish to risk provoking physical violence. In particular, people who have been physically injured by their spouses or another individual in the past should probably not use Self Mediation with that person. Instead, counseling and/or legal remedies are advised.

Prerequisite #5:

Power Is Not Severely Unbalanced, *and*
Neither Person Characteristically Abuses Power

Power is a characteristic of relationships, not of individuals. It is the capacity of one person to influence the behavior of the Other. This ability to influence the Other's behavior is related directly to the strength of the Other's needs. If Juan desperately needs Karen's support, then Karen is able to induce Juan to make concessions.

Power is nearly always mutual – each can affect the other. Hardly ever is one entirely powerless, although at times we may feel so because we fail to recognize our options.

Just because the power in your relationship with your Other is mutual, it is not necessarily balanced. The low-power partner (the one with the greatest needs of the Other), is most vulnerable in the Dialogue. Especially when power imbalance is great, your Other's promise to comply with Cardinal Rule #2 (No Power-plays) is critically important. If you cannot trust the Other to accept this Cardinal Rule and not use the power at his disposal, then entering into a Dialogue might be risky.

Personality factor: *Sadism*

Some people derive pleasure from using power gratuitously to hurt others who are relatively helpless to respond. A pattern of such behavior is called sadism. Sadistic behavior is often associated with low self-esteem. That is, behaving sadistically produces a pleasurable feeling of power that compensates for their feelings of powerlessness and inadequacy.

For example, let's say you are in conflict with your boss and are wondering whether to suggest a meeting to talk it out. You know from past experience that she fires people for "making waves" or punishes "trouble-makers" by assigning undesirable tasks. She then likes to make a public display of the punishment around the office as an example to others. Your boss seems to enjoy wielding coercive, manipulative power. If you have no recourse to protect yourself from or deter her possible abuses, then using Self Mediation may not be prudent.

Another example: Your wife receives a paycheck while you, caring for small children, are not employed outside the home. Let's say that your wife controls all family finances and gives you a weekly amount to buy food. Further, let's say that in the past your wife has withheld the food allowance so that you and the children do not have enough to eat. As in the case of impulsiveness, professional help is recommended.

These two examples illustrate both power imbalance and sadistic abuse of power, as well as uncertain commitment to Cardinal Rule #2. If your Other has both the *ability* and *willingness* to coerce or intimidate you into submission to his demands, then using Self Mediation is risky. The method requires that both partners act according to the Cardinal Rules. Both participants must be willing to forego using coercive force, and to engage in the Dialogue as an alternative way of managing your differences.

Prerequisite #6:

Neither Person Is Addicted to a Chemical Substance

People who are alcoholic or dependent on other drugs suffer from a condition that jeopardizes the success of Self Mediation. Certainly, holding a Dialogue would be pointless if either person is intoxicated or under the influence of drugs. But the dependency does not vanish just because the person is not intoxicated at the time. The dependency syndrome itself impairs the method by disabling certain of the psychological forces toward harmony.

Personality factor: *Addictive Disorder*

People having the so-called "addictive personality" often hear an internal script telling them, "Nothing is ever enough." A desperate need to become satiated drives their compulsive consumption of the substance of their addiction. The problem this chronic hunger poses for Self Mediation is that an addictive Other will be difficult to satisfy with any amount of conciliation. The moment of Breakthrough will then be very difficult, perhaps impossible, to reach. The addicted person (who is not recovering or in treatment) may complicate the process by employing the "covering up" behavior habitually used in hiding the addiction from family and associates.

Prerequisite #7:

Neither Person Suffers from
Severe Emotional Disturbance

"Emotional disturbance" is a loose collection of personality factors that impinge on the effectiveness of Self Mediation. In particular, people who are acutely *paranoid* (a neurosis or psychosis) or *sociopathic* (a character disorder) have distorted perceptions of their relationships that make using the method ill-advised.

All of us employ defenses against anxiety that distort our perceptions of social reality. So even normal, well-adjusted people may occasionally exhibit behavioral symptoms similar to paranoia or sociopathy. These normal ego-defenses are especially likely during periods of high stress.

But this so-called "normal neurosis" does not disable Self Mediation. Most people who have emotional problems severe enough to render the Dialogue ineffective have some history of psychiatric hospitalization or closely supervised outpatient treatment. Our personality quirks and maladjustments are most apparent to the people closest to us. Just because your Other may sometimes seem "crazy" does not mean the method will not work.

You may consider yourself unqualified to assess whether these emotional disturbances are present in your Other. Even if you are in doubt, you can probably try Self Mediation without great risk. If it doesn't work for these reasons, damage is not likely. Your Dialogue will simply be another frustrating argument that may seem not unlike many previous encounters.

Prerequisite #8:

Both People Speak a Common Language

Rarely could two people have an ongoing interdependent relationship in workplace or home settings who do not regularly communicate in a common language. However, if Clashes between people who cannot communicate verbally were to arise, Self Mediation would be difficult to carry out. After all, the Dialogue does entail face-to-face communication.

All Of The Above

After reading this chapter, you may be thinking, "All of my conflicts are with sociopathic, sadistic, paranoid drug addicts who have me trapped under their thumb." If such a thought discourages you from using Self Mediation in a relationship that matters to you, refresh your understanding of the Bad Person Illusion in chapter 4.

Part 4

THIRD-PARTY MEDIATION

Chapter 16:

HELPING OTHERS MANAGE THEIR DIFFERENCES

Writers in the field of dispute resolution define mediation in various ways. Without known exception, every definition involves a *third* party – someone other than the disputants themselves. Here is a fairly conventional way of understanding mediation:

> *"The role of a neutral third party in facilitating the search for mutually acceptable, self-determined agreements between two or more disputants "*

But you have noticed that Self Mediation does not involve a third party. Rather, the essential functions of a neutral third party are incorporated into the role of the initiator of the method. So, the initiator plays two roles:
   1) Negotiator – an advocate of her own self-interests
   2) Mediator – an advocate of both-gain solution to the disputed issues

All of us occasionally observe conflicts between others in which we are not "principal" parties – that is, we are not personally in dispute. Yet, we may have some responsibility for, or interest in, the outcome. Managers need their employees to work together collaboratively, but have no personal stake in the issues that they dispute. Parents want their children to cooperate, but are not personally invested in what the kids are arguing about.

This chapter explains how the four steps of Self Mediation can be reframed so we can act as a neutral third party to help others manage their differences. Since it is not really a "do-it-yourself" process when applied by a third party, we will refer to it in this chapter as "Simple Mediation."

The Active-Passive Debate

In mediation, as in other professional fields, practitioners disagree. One debate among mediators concerns how active or passive the mediator should be during meetings with disputants. That is, does success depend on the substantive contributions of the mediator (the "active mediator" argument)? Or, does success arise from factors other than the mediator's expert knowledge about the substantive issues in dispute (the "passive mediator" argument)? If a combination, in what proportion do these two elements contribute to success in finding solutions?

An important consideration in the active-passive debate is the "structure" of the parties. Structure refers to
- the *size* of the parties – whether they are individuals, groups, organizations or nations;
- the *number* of separate contesting parties; and
- the *degree of consensus* of opinion within each party that permits it to speak with one voice through a leader or representative.

The Simplest Structure

Forms of mediation are applied to complex structures, such as negotiating international peace treaties, and developing a company's strategic plan that involves several department heads. Mediation is also used with two individuals, such as co-workers and marital partners. Clearly, the two-person relationship has the most simple structure possible.

Simple Mediation can be simple because it is designed specifically for managing differences only in two-person relationships. Applying the method to more complex situations calls for careful attention to the implications of other structural features, which falls outside the scope of this book.

Where Does Resolution Come From?

Back to the active-passive debate for a moment. The argument reduces to this basic question: "Are the forces that lead to resolution of interpersonal conflict introduced by the mediator, or do they exist within the pair relationship itself?" If the mediator produces the resolution, then the forces are external to the pair – this requires active mediation. If the resolution evolves as a natural product of communication between the parties under the special environment that mediation provides, then the forces are internal to the pair – this permits passive mediation.

My experience, as well as substantial research and theory in behavioral science, suggests that passive mediation works best when structure is simple. That is, the forces that lead to resolution of two-person conflicts are resident in the relationship between the partners, ready to come forth when conditions are favorable. Mediation is an opportunity for structured communication that allows those forces to emerge and take effect. These are described in detail in Chapter 19: "Forces Toward Harmony."

The Role of the Mediator

So, we conclude that passive mediation is effective in resolving two-person conflicts. Since we recognize that Self Mediation can produce interpersonal peace without a third party, you might be wondering, "Of what use, then, is a mediator?"

A third party can perform several useful functions that help Simple Mediation resolve disputes more effectively than when the four-step method is applied as Self Mediation, which involves only the two disputing parties:

1) A reluctant disputant can be more effectively persuaded to participate if the Dialogue is proposed by a third party than if proposed by her opponent. The mistrustful climate of most interpersonal conflicts leads one to suspect that her Other is driven by manipulative, self-serving motives in suggesting that they meet to discuss contested issues. When proposed by a neutral mediator who has no personal stake in the outcome, this suspiciousness and distrust is minimized.

2) The mediator can exercise more control in ensuring that a participant who becomes frustrated with the process will not break Cardinal Rule #1 by withdrawing or walking out. When the Dialogue is under way without a mediator, the person who has initiated it is vulnerable to his Other's reneging on the commitment to stay in the meeting until it is concluded. A mediator can more forcefully insist that a wavering participant stay in the room and continue discussion.

3) The mediator can exercise more control in ensuring that neither partner violates Cardinal Rule #2 by employing coercive force or intimidating threats to defeat her foe. Indeed, some lopsided power conflicts may be resolvable only by involving a third party.

4) The mediator, being less emotionally involved, can listen more attentively for conciliatory gestures. When such a gesture occurs, the mediator can bring attention to it with a comment like "It sounded like you made an offer to compromise a moment ago. Could you say more about that?" or "Did you notice that Rae said she felt bad for you?" This kind of supportive attention can be difficult for a participant to give, especially when he is angry.

5) When the Breakthrough occurs, the mediator can more effectively help frame an agreement than if deal-making is left to the partners. The mediator may be able to think more clearly about the necessary elements of a behaviorally specific agreement than can a participant who remains emotionally upset. Also, urgings by a mediator to correct a flaw in an agreement are met with less defensive resistance than when weak spots are noted by a foe.

6) Finally, a mediator can make use of what social psychologists call the "audience effect" in following up with participants at some agreed time in the future. The audience effect accounts for why participants feel more obligated to a neutral third party in living up to their part of an agreement than they do to their counterpart in conflict. Follow-up by the mediator typically consists of:

    A) Meeting again with the participants at a specific time agreed to by all at the close of the Dialogue.

B) Asking at the follow-up meeting, "How is it working?" to prompt the participants to review the agreement.

C) Helping to fine tune the agreement if necessary.

D) Congratulating the partners on their successful efforts to bring harmony to their relationship.

Who Can Mediate?

Simple Mediation is generic. That is, it can be used to resolve any two-person conflict that meets the prerequisites in chapter 15. The only requirements of the mediator who employs the process are that she

1) is accepted by both participants into the third party role. This acceptance is most likely when the mediator

2) is perceived by each partner as

   A) relatively neutral and unbiased, meaning that she is not an advocate of either person, and

   B) having some base of power to enter the role of third party with the two people in conflict. This power can reside in either

   a) being perceived as a competent mediator, or

   b) having authority to require that a Dialogue occur, even if one or both participants are reluctant to meet.

3) refrain from interfering with the Essential Process during the Dialogue. Mediators are best able to avoid this common mistake who

   A) know the procedure of Simple Mediation,

B) understand some of the behavioral science
that explains how the method produces
harmony, and

C) have confidence that the method works.

Low-Skill Mediation?

Many people are surprised by how little skill and
knowledge are required of the mediator. Surprise may arise from
the popular belief that the mediator's personal abilities account
for more of the results of mediation than is argued here.

On a cautionary note, however, I recommend that you at
least be experienced in using the four-step method as Self
Mediation before undertaking a third party effort. Although it is
simple to understand, pitfalls can trip the new mediator that only
experience can teach her to avoid. I am reminded of the saying,
"Good judgment comes from experience; experience comes from
bad judgment." Give yourself several opportunities to practice
bad judgment in Self Mediation before offering your good
judgment to others.

If you are now a mediator who holds different beliefs
about your role than those presented here, I do not expect you to
be convinced so readily that some of your favorite mediation
tools are less than vital. And, please remember that Self
Mediation, and its Simple Mediation variant, are designed for
self-help, not for professional service. I do not suggest that more
complex and demanding mediation tools may not be helpful and

at times required. Mediators are eagerly invited to test this simple model and report their experiences to me c/o the publisher.

Managerial Mediation

As long as the basic mediator requirements spelled out above are met, then mediators can assist pairs of people wherever they find them. Simple Mediation can help people manage differences and build better relationships in several sectors of life.

Workplace conflict is of special interest. For over fifteen years I have developed and promoted Simple Mediation as a powerful form of participative management – called "Managerial Mediation." Increasingly, managers and team leaders are using mediation to solve productivity problems resulting from poor communication and cooperation between employees – estimated to account for 65% of job performance deficiency.

Clearly it is impractical to train managers extensively in mediation techniques – managing workplace conflict is rarely a primary job function. Nevertheless, managers can learn Simple Mediation by reading this book or attending a one-day presentation of the Manager-as-Mediator Seminar – a very cost-effective investment in people-skills for the workplace.

Managers hold a significant advantage, compared with mediators who are not in roles of authority. If necessary, the manager can override employees' reluctance to participate by pointing to the impact on productivity resulting from their difficulty in working cooperatively. Because the managerial mediation session is a business meeting, not a discussion of personal issues, it is a powerful means of solving organizational problems.

Non-supervisory staff may also apply Simple Mediation in the workplace – personnel specialists, employee relations staff, internal organization development consultants, employee assistance program counselors, and training consultants. And, Simple Mediation is an especially useful skill for members of self-directed work teams.

The Better Way

The field of mediation has expanded tremendously since 1980. Modern society is discovering that there is a better way to resolve conflicts than the means that we have relied upon throughout history. Although forms of third party intervention in disputes have existed for centuries, the need has never been greater than now for peaceful ways to manage human differences.

Part 5

WHY IT WORKS

Chapter 17:

INTRODUCTION TO
THE BEHAVIORAL SCIENCE OF
DIFFERENCE-MANAGEMENT

As discussed in chapter 2, Self Mediation is a behavioral prescription. Follow the prescription, and reap the results. It works, even if you don't know the theory that explains why it works.

So why is a section about behavioral science included in this book? Some readers are mediators, consultants, students, and academicians who have a professional interest in theories of difference-management. Other readers just enjoy learning new ways of understanding their own behavior.

If you have no professional or academic interest in this field, but simply would like practical guidance in building better relationships, you might choose to skip ahead to chapter 21. Just use Self Mediation as it has already been presented. But those of you whose interest extends beyond a personal one will find Part 5 of the book of special benefit.

Mental Maps

Each one of us has, whether or not we are aware of it, a "mental map" that guides our behavior throughout each day. A mental map is a system of beliefs and assumptions that provides a sense of orderliness and predictability in our personal worlds. Our mental maps provide the basis of the hundreds of automatic decisions about how to act that we make each day. Your mental map differs from mine because our past experiences have been different, giving us different assumptions about how to behave in the world in order to get what we want from it.

When we are interacting with others, we are behaving. We are acting and reacting, talking and responding. Our behavior is not random. It is ordered and purposeful to the extent that our mental maps guide our behavior. We assume, whether correctly or not, that acting in a particular way will produce an intended outcome. If I am yelling at you, it is because I assume that "Impressing on you the strength of my anger will cause you to give in to me." If I walk out and slam the door, my mental map has led me to believe that "Showing you how hurt I am will make you feel sorry for me, and then you will let me have my way" or perhaps "Conflicts are hopeless; it's best to avoid them."

These internal scripts come from past experiences that taught us lessons. Each of these old lessons (many of which may not have come from good teachers) provided information that today make up parts of our mental maps about how to manage interpersonal differences.

This information establishes a causal ("if-then") link between behavioral options and the likely consequences of each option. Since we generally attempt to behave in ways that will promote our own self-interests, these if-then links constitute a chain of assumptions that guide our way toward desired outcomes.

Revising Our Mental Maps

Scientifically sound theories, models, and concepts supply accurate information about how to behave when in conflict. Learning valid models helps us revise parts of our mental maps so that they serve as more reliable guides to where we want to go – satisfying, productive, harmonious relationships. For example, the part of my map that says "Walking out will make you feel sorry for me" might change to "Walking out will only deepen your resentment toward me and make it harder to resolve this." This changed if-then link in my map will cause me to act differently in future conflicts.

This chapter introduces the behavioral science of difference-management. The concepts and models that follow come to us from several disciplines – particularly psychology, sociology, communication theory, organizational behavior, cultural anthropology, and ethology. I have made no attempt to be comprehensive in reviewing relevant scientific literature, nor to report research from original sources. Rather, I have synthesized information from several fields that helps us understand the anatomy of interpersonal differences and how they can be managed constructively. Although most of this information is accepted scientific theory, some ideas are somewhat controversial. Certain parts are my own informed speculation that I hope the reader will regard as worthy of consideration. Whether they be proven facts or the subjects of informed debate, the ideas presented here will add more detail to your mental map.

Chapter 18:

DYNAMICS OF INTERPERSONAL CONFLICT

Interpersonal conflict is a system of behavior. Like other complex systems, it is comprised of many interrelated subsystems that contain elements that interact dynamically. In this chapter, we will look at four relevant dynamics of interpersonal conflict:

- *Issues in conflict*
- *The retaliatory cycle*
- *Confrontation and conciliation phases*
- *The ambivalence-projection-polarization chain*

ISSUES IN CONFLICT

"Issues" may be thought of as "matters of concern" to participants. In every conflict, there are three kinds of issues that concern the parties: *substantive, emotional,* and *pseudo-substantive.*

Substantive Issues

Unless you and your Other have jointly adopted a policy of non-communication to cope with your differences, you have arguments. Your arguments are about issues, the matters of mutual concern. You may argue with your spouse about how to handle money, or about whose career is more important. You may argue with a co-worker about whose turn it is to answer the phones, or with your boss about whether your performance review was properly conducted, or with your teenage child about what time to come home from the school dance. The subjects of these arguments are "substantive issues." Taken at face value, substantive issues are matters that concern the participants and therefore are the problem to be solved or the question to be decided.

Positions

Each partner holds a position on the disputed substantive issue that differs from the position held by the Other. You think monthly budgeting is the proper method of handling family finances; your spouse believes that keeping track of the checking account balance and exercising self-restraint while shopping is a more practical approach. You think your job performance merits a satisfactory rating; your boss insists that it calls for an unsatisfactory evaluation. You want your teenager home from the dance by 11:00; she wants to stay out until midnight. Your statements during the argument are attempts to persuade the Other to accept your position, and vice versa.

At this time, let me introduce you to Jane, an unnoticed observer of these arguments. Jane assumes that resolving a conflict is simply a matter of finding a mutually acceptable compromise position on the substantive issues being argued, or possibly finding some previously unrecognized alternative position that satisfies both participants' self-interests. Be forewarned: Jane is in for an education in the next few pages.

Emotional Issues

After some reflection on what she witnessed during your latest argument, Jane notices that the conflict was not simply a difference of opinion – a reasonable, unemotional discussion. An unemotional difference of opinion is distinctly different from a tense or angry encounter. The latter is what we call a "conflict." A mere difference of opinion is seldom regarded as a problem – just a subject for conversation. The angry argument she observed was clearly not just a conversation.

Noticing this distinction helps Jane to recognize that when people are in conflict, emotional matters of concern must also be involved – we will call these concerns "emotional issues."

Personal Needs and Emotional Issues

What might be the emotional issues in a conflict between spouses about handling money, or between you and your boss about the accuracy of your performance appraisal? Emotional issues fall into a rather small number of categories:

1) Issues of POWER, deriving from individual needs for control and influence over others, and for the social status created by power differences.
2) Issues of APPROVAL, deriving from individual needs for affection – to be liked.
3) Issues of INCLUSION, deriving from individual needs for acceptance into social groups.
4) Issues of JUSTICE, deriving from individual needs to be treated fairly, equally and equitably.

5) Issues of IDENTITY, deriving from individual needs
for autonomy, self-esteem, positive self-image, self-
determination and affirmation of personal values.

Whether these categories are exhaustive or mutually
exclusive is unimportant. Our point here is that emotional issues
underlie arguments about substantive issues. Indeed, the
presence of emotional issues is what distinguishes a "conflict"
from a "disagreement." That is, substantive issues are felt to be
important only to the extent that they are vehicles for the
resolution of emotional issues.

To Know Thyself

Emotional issues are not as easy to recognize as are
substantive issues. In the heat of argumentative battle, we
generally do not mention them. Perhaps especially in the
workplace, we don't often speak of our needs for power, our
needs to be liked and approved of, or our needs to be socially
included. For better or worse, social and organizational norms
typically discourage open disclosure of these needs. After years
of learning how to fit in, we have incorporated these norms so
deeply that we are often not even consciously aware of our own
emotional issues. Being unaware of them, we have difficulty
"getting in touch" with how we feel and describing these feelings
clearly.

Even so, these fundamental human needs are present in
each of us. So, in every interpersonal dispute, emotional issues
supply the energy that fuels the flames of conflict. They are the
fire in us that our foes try to douse with logical persuasion.

Unbeknownst to the douser, however, our persuasive
efforts to put out the fire are often the emotional equivalent of

gasoline. Attempting to change the Other's mind with facts and logic only increases his conviction that he is right. His personal needs that spawn emotional issues cannot be reduced or satisfied through persuasion, argument, or logical reasoning. On the contrary, we cling ever more dearly to our positions as the Other refuses to recognize the superior logic of our position. His stubborn resistance to accepting our position on the substantive issue only lends further evidence to our belief that he is wrong. The heat of battle intensifies.

Remember Jane, our scientifically curious observer? She can now identify the substantive and emotional issues in the conflicts she witnessed a while ago. She recognizes that each spouse in the money conflict needs to feel in control of the family's financial resources (an issue of power). She recognizes that the employee's needs to be treated fairly and to maintain a positive self-concept as a competent worker are violated by the boss's evaluation of his performance (issues of justice and identity). Similarly, the teenager needs to be viewed by her peers as having matured beyond childish curfews (issues of identity, approval, and inclusion).

We might conclude that conflict resolution is achieved by bringing emotional issues out of the protective darkness of silence, and into the light of open discussion. Not so fast, Jane cautions. There is more to understand.

With ever-increasing insight, Jane notices that disputants often become reconciled, resolved, conciliatory, more trusting, and more intimate without having come to a specific agreement on the substantive issue they were arguing about. Even more surprisingly, the emotional needs underlying the substantive

issues may not have been directly addressed and resolved. This
is puzzling. If not by a reasoned exchange of views on the
contested issues, how do conflicts become resolved?

Pseudo-substantive Issues

Jane has noticed a curious phenomenon that may provide
a clue to the answer. She observes that during arguments,
additional issues are brought up and disputed. The contesters
then stake out opposing positions on these new issues and treat
them as though they are substantive. Often, these additional,
apparently substantive issues had not been mentioned previously.
Sometimes, they are awakened from a hibernation that began in a
previous season of the partners' relationship.

Jane has also noticed that, when reconciliation
eventually does occur, many of these new subjects of argument
are ignored – no agreement is reached on them. How can this
happen? Were these substantive issues actually unimportant? Is
reconciling different positions on substantive issues actually
unnecessary? If so, what was the argument really about? Jane
begins to suspect that the process of solving conflicts is not as
logical as she had first assumed.

A Deception of Self and Other

Jane's suspicions are correct. The "substantive" issues
being argued were not as substantive as they appeared at face
value. Having one's preferred position accepted by the Other
was not all that mattered – perhaps this was not even a
significant concern. The apparently substantive issues were, to
some degree, "pseudo-substantive." That is, they were partially
or even wholly false, not materially related to the disputants'

objective underlying interests. But why are pseudo-substantive issues present in conflicts? What purpose do they serve?

Issues are substantive to the extent that they represent objective, rational underlying self-interests. Issues are pseudo-substantive to the extent that they serve to satisfy individual needs related to emotional issues. So, any disputed issue can be, and usually is, both substantive and pseudo-substantive.

To summarize how the three kinds of issues are related:

Pseudo-substantive issues
are **emotional** *issues*
disguised as **substantive** *issues.*

Jane is dismayed. How can two people in conflict ever sort out rational self-interest from unconsciously generated pseudo-substantive issues? Fortunately, recalling chapter 13, Jane recognizes that resolution is not rational – "The problem does not have to be solved for the conflict to be resolved." The remainder of Part 5 will guide Jane's rational mind through this paradox.

Illustration

Let's consider the case of Roger who disputes his most recent performance evaluation by his boss, Donna. Roger's somewhat negative evaluation is of substantive concern to him to the extent that his salary and career progress may be affected. It is pseudo-substantive to the extent that it affects his self-esteem, status among co-workers, and feelings of being treated fairly. In the proportion that it affects both, the issue is both substantive and pseudo-substantive.

But this is not the first time that Roger has felt he was treated unfairly by his boss. Previous instances of perceived unfair treatment produced feelings of resentment but the issues were never discussed with Donna. These old resentments have accumulated to form a pool of "angry energy" in Roger's subterranean psyche. The negative performance evaluation raises the level of the pool to overflowing. He shouts angrily at her.

The display of anger directed at Donna is not in proportion to the severity of this particular insult – the somewhat negative evaluation. Roger's pent-up anger requires venting far beyond what is an appropriate response to the present issue. In order to dissipate leftover anger, Roger criticizes other areas that are not related to the immediate problem – her sketchy technical knowledge, out-dated style of dress, and overall incompetence as a manager (pseudo-substantive issues). He is discharging anger from the reservoir within.

Some of these pseudo-substantive issues have some actual impact on Roger's self-interest; others are entirely irrelevant. But he himself is unaware of this. He is deceiving himself into believing that the pseudo-substantive issues are actually substantive. The conflict between Roger and Donna compounds as Roger expresses these criticisms of Donna to other employees, creating tension and contaminating others' relationships with her.

The self-deception inherent in pseudo-substantive issues is unconscious and reflexive, not premeditated or consciously intended. Although past experience has shaped how we do it, the psychological mechanism that creates pseudo-substantive issues is inherited. It is a psycho-biological process that we are born with and will have until we die, and will genetically pass on to our children. It is human nature. By learning new skills and gaining new insights into behavior we can manage our behavior more constructively, but we cannot eliminate the process within us that creates pseudo-substantive issues.

Implications

How does our understanding of the three kinds of issues guide us in managing interpersonal differences?

- Managing differences does not necessarily require agreement to be reached on any particular substantive issue. Disputed issues may be largely pseudo-substantive, having little impact on objective underlying self-interests. To that degree, compromises and concessions may be easily exchanged between participants.
- Conflict resolution requires the discharge of angry energy accumulated from prior frustration.
- Participants in conflict cannot be expected to act reasonably or logically until angry energy has been discharged.

THE RETALIATORY CYCLE

Periodically, an event triggers conflict which evidences itself through an exchange of hostile behaviors. We commonly refer to this exchange as a "fight."

For example, the triggering event may be a comment by a spouse during dinner that a checking account overdraft notice came in the mail. This seemingly innocent bit of information launches the couple into another fight over the best style of managing money. As the argument continues, accusations, self-defensive explanations, attacks and counter-attacks are exchanged. The couple is engaged in a "retaliatory cycle."

Figure 1: *Retaliatory Cycle*

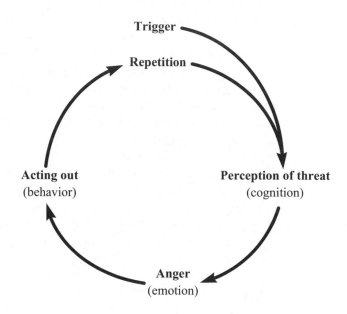

The sequence of events in the retaliatory cycle are as follows:

1) *Triggering event.* Any verbal or non-verbal behavior by Person A. May be intended as hostile, or purely innocent.
2) *Perception of threat.* Person B perceives that his self-interest is at risk. Can arise from inferring hostile intent ("She is trying to sabotage me"), or simply from carelessness ("You inconsiderate nincompoop!"). This is the <u>cognitive</u> component of the cycle.

3) *Defensive anger.* The natural and automatic emotional response to perceiving that one is being attacked. Anger is the mobilization of energy to protect oneself, and is entirely healthy. This is the emotional component of the cycle.

4) *Acting out.* Unless its energy is harnessed for constructive problem-solving, Person B's defensive anger is transformed into self-protective behavior – either Coercion or Distancing. Coercion with Power-plays leads to "spiraling up" toward escalation, retaliation, and even violence. Distancing with Walk-aways leads to "spiraling down" toward lessened interdependency, impoverishment of the relationship, and even divorce or termination. Either form of acting out is an unconscious *strategy,* biologically designed by evolution to ensure our survival of dangerous situations. This is the behavioral component of the cycle.

5) *Repetition.* Person B's acting out may be perceived by Person A as an unprovoked triggering event. This sequence then becomes an endless loop from which there is no natural escape. Each participant feels unable to safely stop the cycle without accepting defeat.

This is the anatomy of a fight.

Living and working in highly social groups, we can and usually do exercise self-control in preventing the retaliatory cycle from escalating to violence, typically by Distancing enough to avoid provoking retaliation. Unfortunately, Walk-aways cause our relationships to spiral down, depriving us of the pleasure and benefits that they could potentially give us. And, there are many tragic occasions, some reported in the headlines, where Coercion has been the defensive strategy of choice, resulting in spiraling up to violence.

Regardless of how successfully we exercise self-control over our behavior, the retaliatory cycle is psychologically primitive in origin, and is biologically rooted in our ancient past. The reflexes are powerful and are not fully controlled by willpower. The retaliatory cycle is a typical, even universal, form of interaction during interpersonal conflicts.

Implications

How does understanding the mechanics of the retaliatory cycle help us manage differences? During the Dialogue of Self Mediation,

- We can "reality test" our assumptions about our Other's intentions, checking them for accuracy. We might discover that a triggering event was not motivated by hostility after all, or that it was an unavoidable mistake that the Other regrets. Consequently, we short-circuit the retaliatory cycle, preventing it from spiraling up or down toward ruin.
- We can apply Cardinal Rule #1 to outlaw Walk-aways. Withdrawing from communication is often experienced by others as a hostile tactic. Mutual Distancing is an "armed standoff" that deprives each participant of satisfaction of needs. This uneasy truce only temporarily suspends the retaliatory cycle; it does not stop the fight. Cardinal Rule #1 reinstates communication, the lifeblood of resolution.
- We can apply Cardinal Rule #2 to outlaw Power-plays. Coercion or intimidation to force compliance with demands causes conflict to spiral up toward violence. Force begets force. Each increase in the

level of force brings a corresponding increase in retaliation by the Other. With each escalating round of the cycle, the stakes are raised for each participant, making it ever more difficult to find a face-saving way to escape from the cycle.

CONFRONTATION AND CONCILIATION PHASES

Most of us can recall a "good fight" with a spouse that somehow led to intimacy, or a "frank discussion" with a colleague that resulted in renewed trust and cooperation, or a "heart-to-heart talk" with an offended friend that brought the return of warmth and mutual support.

We can also recall many episodes of the retaliatory cycle that left us upset and angry. On such occasions, a reservoir of angry energy remained within us, tugging at our self-restraint, demanding an outlet.

What accounts for the difference between these two experiences? Why do fights sometimes lead to resolution, and at other times bring only frustration? Often, the difference is whether the fight was permitted to continue through completion of the "confrontation" phase and proceed to the "conciliation" phase of the encounter.

Hydraulic Theory of Emotion

Eons of interpersonal conflict have contributed popular expressions to modern language that describe this experience: "letting off steam," "getting things off your chest," "blowing your top." These phrases suggest a "hydraulic theory" of emotion, indicating that pressure contained within a closed system seeks release through some outlet.

The validity of the hydraulic theory of emotion is debated among behavioral scientists. Whether or not you subscribe to the theory, the indisputable fact is that time for confrontation within an appropriate context normally precedes emotional readiness to reconcile. An analogy of the confrontation and conciliation phases is illustrated as the "Conflict Mountain":

Figure 2: *Conflict Mountain*

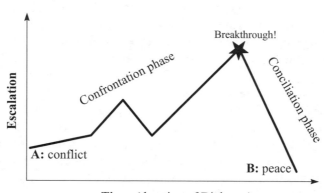

Time (duration of Dialogue)

Join me in plotting a journey. Imagine that you are at point "A" and wish to travel to point "B." Between you and your destination stands a mountain. No road bypasses the mountain, so you must travel up to the peak, then down. So it is impossible to get to "B" without enduring the difficult part of the journey, the upward climb. Nor is it possible to go down before going up. "A" precedes "B." This is an inescapable fact, like it or not.

Point "A" represents a state of unresolved conflict with your Other. You wish that your relationship were harmonious and satisfying, rather than tense and uncomfortable. These objectives lie at your destination, point "B." The "conflict mountain" stands between you and your goal. The stressful upward journey that you must travel first is the confrontation phase; the easier downward part is the conciliation phase.

You wish that you could magically find yourself at peace with your Other. But magic is not of the natural world. Human nature (psychology) is a part of the world, just as "mountain nature" (geology) is also part of the world. The height of the mountain symbolizes the amount of escalation necessary before one can proceed to reconciliation. You may have to scale the mountain to intimidating heights. Also, it is not a journey you can travel alone, at your own pace; you can only go there with your Other. You are interdependent, as if handcuffed together.

Often, when we find ourselves at point "A" and aspire to point "B," our fear of confronting the Other is so great that we hardly get started before we quit the climb. Our dread is magnified by being unable to see the top of the mountain. Its height is uncertain, but looking up from the bottom, the peak looms frighteningly high. We believe that danger lurks at high altitudes and that we, as individuals or as a relationship, might be hurt if we climb too high.

Another apprehension about starting to climb together is that past experiences have revealed the Other's habit is to quit part way up, leaving us up there all alone. So, we often take the safe option of not starting the climb at all.

But climbing the mountain is the *only* way to get to point "B." We sometimes try to act as if we are already at point "B," doing our best to act polite. But triggering events remind us that we really aren't there yet. So, we wait beside the mountain, making tentative starts from time to time, feeling helplessly dependent on the other to show signs of trustworthiness, or hoping that some magical vehicle will transport us effortlessly to point "B."

Implications

The existence of confrontation and conciliation phases of the Dialogue means that:
- It is necessary to engage in confrontation before we can expect resolution and harmony.
- It is necessary to ensure that neither partner will abandon the journey before reaching point "B."

The risk of harm to the relationship posed by escalation is real, but is perceptually exaggerated. It may be helpful to set some groundrules for the Dialogue that will prevent the escalation from being greater than necessary.

AMBIVALENCE, PROJECTION, AND POLARIZATION

Because the world is not simple and best answers are not easy to find, we are ambivalent about most things. That is, we have few feelings, needs or wishes that are not incongruent with other feelings, needs and wishes. We may like our jobs, but we also find our jobs frustrating and stressful. We may love our spouse, but may also find him/her annoying and perhaps sometimes even hateful.

Few wishes or needs are so simple that we are not ambivalent about them. Certainly our feelings toward the significant Others in our lives are not uniformly positive. We feel both attraction and repulsion, liking and dislike, respect and disrespect.

Cognitive Dissonance

Having two incompatible experiences at the same time is inherently uncomfortable, an experience that psychologists call "cognitive dissonance." Our inner workings strive to reduce dissonance and replace it with consonance.

For example, Howard considers himself a wise shopper, yet he recently spent $40,000 on an automobile that requires frequent mechanical service. The two experiences, "I am a wise shopper" and "I bought a lemon," are incompatible. Howard attempts to regain cognitive consonance by adjusting his perceptions so that the two conflicting experiences are no longer in conflict. In this case, he might tell himself, "Expensive cars are complex hi-tech machines, so it takes awhile to work out the bugs. It will all be worth it in the end." This rationalization permits Howard to retain his positive self-concept as a wise shopper in the face of evidence that he made an unwise purchase. These attitude adjustments almost always take place unconsciously and automatically.

Ambivalence, as it occurs in conflict, often produces cognitive dissonance. When we are ambivalent about a particular substantive issue, we are not entirely "of one mind." We may not be absolutely certain what to believe, or which position to support on a complex issue. Recognizing some truth in two alternative positions, both of which cannot be correct, is inherently discomforting and stressful.

To illustrate these dynamics, let's sit in on a project team meeting at the Hard Core Manufacturing Company. The team is discussing two options: (1) to delay production of a new widget in order to ensure quality, or (2) to meet the deadline in spite of likely quality problems. Each of these two positions has both merits and drawbacks.

Projection

As a member of the team, Helen is unsure which position to espouse. Her uneasy ambivalence seeks resolution. Here, dissonance is the anxiety aroused by Helen's awareness of not knowing an answer and, at the same time, thinking of herself as a smart person. The ego-defense mechanism of "projection" provides a way for Helen to reduce the tension of cognitive dissonance caused by ambivalence, and to achieve consonance.

When we "project," we attribute some undesired characteristic of ourselves to another person. That is, we see it in the Other rather than in ourselves. By projecting this characteristic onto the Other, it is eliminated from ourselves, and so our dissonance is reduced.

Projecting to Reduce Ambivalence

Projection is a mechanism for lowering the ambivalence that arouses dissonance. By attributing one side of our ambivalence about some issue onto another person, we can then perceive the Other as supporting a belief or position that we reject.

Let's say that to reduce her ambivalence about the issue before her team, Helen chooses to champion position #1, to delay production. Once her choice is made, Helen feels relieved of ambivalence by achieving resolution on the issue.

How do we decide which side of our ambivalence to support and which side to project, if not on the objective merits of the two positions? Helen's choice to support position #1 is somewhat arbitrary because the data, which would conclusively prove which option is better, are incomplete. All important decisions are made under conditions of uncertainty – otherwise they would be easy and we would all agree. But once the choice is made, our human egos demand that "that which is me" is favored over "that which is not me." Once projected, the denied part of herself – the "not me" part – becomes inherently negative, undesirable. Helen's adaptive mind then goes to work unconsciously rearranging her analysis of information about the issue so that she views the rejected position (to not delay) as a bad idea. She now regards it as worthless scrap that is cast off from her "rational" analysis. A decision has been made, although it may not be the best decision.

From *Intra*personal to *Inter*personal Conflict

This mental maneuvering removes Helen's ambivalence and thereby reduces her cognitive dissonance. That is, it resolves her *intra*personal conflict – the conflict within herself. But reducing ambivalence through projection has a troubling side effect: It creates *inter*personal conflict.

Helen's intrapsychic peace, won by this self-manipulation, is short-lived. A few moments later in the team meeting, her colleague, John, while exploring pros and cons of the two options, points out a merit of position #2, that production should not be delayed. In making this comment, John unwittingly threatens Helen's new-found intrapsychic harmony – being "of one mind" – and presents himself as a convenient target for her projection. Giving John's comment serious consideration would rekindle her ambivalence, so she is obliged to perceive it as an unworthy idea.

John may or may not have reached a decision on the issue – he simply pointed out a bit of data. But Helen has projected onto him the belief that production should not be delayed. She had rejected that position in order to reduce the intrapsychic tension of ambivalence; it is now an unwanted, denied, former part of herself. So she now perceives that John holds that belief, rather than herself. Now, instead of struggling with her internal indecision, Helen can act out the struggle interpersonally. We see the beginning of a two-person conflict.

Regarding herself as a good problem solver, Helen must now protect that part of her self-concept by ensuring that other team members agree with her. As the team's discussion continues, she points out the flaws in John's position. Since the issue of whether to delay is a complex and controversial one, she can use very reasonable and sound arguments in doing so. If Helen can persuade others that she is correct, then she must surely have made the right choice. She convinces herself by convincing others.

Personalization

Like us all, Helen must maintain a positive self-concept. To do so requires that she believe her position is correct. It also leads to her opinion that John's holding an opposite position must mean that he is not only incorrect but also defective in some way. Why else would someone believe something opposite to her belief? Regardless of past assurances that "reasonable people may disagree," our natural ego-defense requirements urge us to assume that people who believe differently from us must be flawed.

So, in order to maintain her cognitive consonance, Helen questions John's competency. He obviously must be uninformed or prejudiced, as demonstrated by his support of a wrong idea. Further ego-protection is achieved by believing that anyone who supports that idea is not only wrong, but is also stupid. Helen has now "personalized" the conflict; that is, she has attributed the reason for their conflict to the personal characteristics of her Other, John.

In projecting and personalizing the conflict, it is Helen's *own* anxieties about being incompetent, uninformed, prejudiced, and stupid that are relieved by seeing those flaws in John.

Meanwhile back in the team meeting, John, being only human, is simultaneously going through the same ambivalence-reduction process across the table from her. His conclusion is that meeting the deadline is the correct solution to the team's problem, and that anyone who thinks otherwise must be stupid. This is the anatomy of a "personality conflict."

Polarization

This mutual projection of rejected positions on substantive issues reduces intrapsychic ambivalence for both John and Helen. But it also leads to polarization. That is, both have projected onto the other the unwanted side of their intrapersonal ambivalence on the issue, and are now arguing about it. Helen's original *intra*personal conflict is now being acted out as an *inter*personal conflict. Since egos cannot permit letting in disconfirming information that would arouse ambivalence, each partner must introduce new data to support the correctness of their respectively preferred positions on the "substantive" issue – largely pseudo-substantive, since it serves as a vehicle for meeting emotional needs. Helen and John have polarized to the extent that they seem to hold totally opposite positions on the issue of whether to meet the production deadline. Agreement now seems increasingly difficult to achieve unless one gives in to the other and accepts defeat. They have created a win-lose conflict.

This ambivalence-projection-polarization chain helps explain the puzzling phenomenon that people who are closest to each other fight the most. Employees may wonder why they ever took a job in an organization full of such crazy, incompetent people. Married couples may constantly fight, leading to the conclusion that they have such opposite personalities, such "irreconcilable differences," that divorce is the only answer.

A gloomy picture? No hope for compatibility? The fact that we sustain long-term, interdependent relationships is testimony to a remarkable ability. Tolerating ambivalence, and refraining from premature projection onto others to defend our egos against the anxiety aroused by intrapsychic ambivalence, is no easy task. Indeed, managing ambivalence may the most highly evolved skill we develop by living and working interdependently with others. Still, especially under stressful conditions, this destructive sequence of events is all too common.

Implications

How does understanding the ambivalence-projection-polarization model help us manage our differences?

- A lengthy period of face-to-face talking may be needed to get each participant's actual positions communicated, to "reality test" projections, leading to recognition that they are inaccurate.
- Conciliatory gestures help to resolve so-called "personality conflicts" by eroding the destructive tendencies to find fault with the Other (personalize)

and exaggerate differences between oneself and the Other (polarize).

- Partners' normal and natural needs to maintain positive self concepts (defense of ego) must be met in ways that do not increase interpersonal conflict. Projection of negative attributes to the Other, which is the typical device for meeting ego-support needs in conflict situations, must be reduced. A both-gain or fair compromise solution to substantive issues must be found, effectively reducing the need to protect the ego from assault.

On To Harmony

This chapter has described several behavioral and mental events that occur during episodes of human conflict. Each of the models contains several elements that interact dynamically. With our understanding of these dynamics, we will next explore the forces that are present in two-person conflicts that Self Mediation harnesses to transform conflict into harmony.

Chapter 19:

FORCES TOWARD HARMONY

Happily, all the psychological dynamics at play in two-person relationships do not promote conflict. Others work in the opposite direction, helping turn conflict into cooperation and tension into harmony.

Once the retaliatory cycle has begun, a key event must happen for resolution of conflict to occur: One of the participants must offer a conciliatory gesture. Someone must indicate a willingness to agree, to compromise, to stop fighting. Without such a gesture, mutual retaliation would continue indefinitely, and the conflict would spiral up or down toward destruction. So before examining the psychological forces toward harmony, let's first sharpen our understanding of the intriguing phenomenon of conciliatory gestures. Then we will look at four forces harnessed by Self Mediation that cause them to happen.

CONCILIATORY GESTURES

Everyone knows from personal experience that not all conflicts are chronic, endless, interpersonal tragedies. Many episodes of the retaliatory cycle result in agreement and renewed trust. How does this transformation take place? The simplest answer is: Conflicts end because conciliatory gestures happen.

What is a conciliatory gesture? As discussed briefly in chapter 10, it is a behavior that signals a shift in attitude from me-against-you to us-against-the-problem. The gesture is usually a verbal statement or question, but can be a non-verbal expression of the same message. It reveals a desire or openness to resolve the conflict in a mutually acceptable way. The element common to all conciliatory gestures is that expressing them is *risky* – it makes one vulnerable to the Other. It presents an opportunity for the Other to score a point in the win-lose game.

Forms of conciliatory gestures are:
- Apologizing
- Expressing regret for one's past behavior
- Conceding on a contested issue
- Offering to compromise
- Expressing empathy for the Other's problems
- Recognizing the legitimacy of the Other's point of view
- Revealing one's own underlying needs and emotional issues
- Disclosing one's thoughts, feelings, motives, and past history as they pertain to the conflict
- Asking for honest feedback
- Expressing positive feelings for the Other, such as affection, admiration, respect
- Accepting personal responsibility for part of the problem
- Initiating search for both gain solutions

Conciliatory gestures often go unnoticed, even by the one who made the gesture. They are skittish creatures that dart cautiously through the shadowy underbrush of the verbal forest. Sometimes they appear as double-entendres whose intended meaning is ambiguous. Indeed, gestures typically surface not as bold, unambiguous statements, but rather as sentiments nested in protective wrapping. To lessen the risk, we combine the conciliatory statement with blaming or critical language within the same sentence.

Often, due to personality or situational factors, one partner is more forthcoming with these gestures than is the Other. But in effectively managed conflict, there eventually is an exchange of conciliatory gestures that promptly results in relaxation of tension, increased affection and intimacy, improved trust. When this welcome moment arrives, the sigh of relief is sometimes audible.

This vital exchange is the Breakthrough part of Self Mediation. The Breakthrough introduces an improved emotional climate that opens a window of opportunity for participants to make a Deal about changes in each one's future behavior that will accommodate the concerns of the Other.

FOUR FORCES

The Breakthrough is the product of several psychological forces harnessed by the Method that act in concert to turn conflict into cooperation, interpersonal war into interpersonal peace. Although other constructive forces may also contribute, this chapter will focus on those that seem most powerful:

- Fatigue
- Desire for peace
- Catharsis
- Inhibitory reflex

Let's explore each of these forces in turn, starting with the most obvious and concrete and moving toward the more obscure and psychodynamic.

Fatigue

People get tired of fighting. Fighting is hard work. We "wear down" and want to stop, to end an unpleasant encounter. Once we see that we cannot "win" the conflict by persuading the Other to accept our demands, we may then see agreeing as the only remaining alternative to continued fighting.

Although it is the most obvious factor, fatigue alone is not sufficient to bring genuine reconciliation. If it were the only influence toward interpersonal peace, then conciliatory gestures would have a shallow tone, sounding like, "Okay, okay, have it your way. Let's agree to something so we can get out of here." Agreements resting only on this foundation would be short-lived at best. But, in combination with the more optimistic forces to follow, fatigue can trigger a participant's willingness to move toward agreement.

Desire for Peace

Being in conflict is inherently unpleasant. Still, many of us perversely seem to like something about it. We all know people who "pick fights" with others for no apparent reason. Let's take a moment to examine this perversity before describing the desire for peace as a force toward harmony.

Early Learning

We learned much as children. Developmental psychologists estimate that our social behavior is mostly determined before we become teenagers, possibly much younger. If our early family environment was characterized by much fighting and arguing, then we learned that conflict is how people connect with other people – the way we get attention from others. Conflict then becomes comfortingly familiar – "better the devil we know than the one we don't." As adults, we reproduce that familiar pattern of social interaction in our own families and workplaces.

Displaced Aggression

Another factor stirs up conflict, causing it to burst spontaneously into flames without reasonable cause. All of us, for periods of time, experience chronic frustration, feeling deprived of satisfactions we believe we are entitled to. Feeling unfairly deprived produces "floating anger" or irritability that lies hidden under the surface of shared waters like a mine awaiting a passing ship. When the mine is inadvertently struck by a co-worker or spouse, it explodes. This explosion is called displaced aggression.

If this mine-laying were conscious or intentional, we would accuse the perpetrator of engaging in interpersonal terrorism. But, since it is unwitting, it is more forgivable. The terrorist, also hurt in the resulting blast, is a victim as well. Still, the innocent victim who happens to be in the wrong place at the wrong time will indignantly protest, "What did I do to deserve this?"

Illustration

A tongue-in-cheek illustration of displaced aggression goes like this:

Janet is criticized by her boss at work one day. Respecting her superiors, she dutifully accepts the criticism without retort. Coming home frustrated after work that night, Janet yells at her spouse, Bill, for not buying groceries on the way home from his day at the office. Bill, hoping to maintain marital harmony, stifles his annoyance and instead spanks their child, Junior, for some minor infraction. Junior, being a well-behaved child, does not retort, but instead kicks the dog, Spot. Spot, being an obedient dog, rather than biting Junior, chases the cat, Kitty. Kitty, recognizing the futility of fighting Spot, kills a mouse. So the mouse pays the ultimate price for Janet's boss criticizing her at work that day.

So, the comfortable familiarity of learned behavior patterns, combined with misdirected aggression arising from floating anger, propel us into episodes of conflict that can seem devoid of rational purpose. At the same time, we find conflict unpleasant, stressful, and noxious. We are torn by a magnet-like duality of attraction and repulsion about conflict. Let's look more closely now at the more positive pole of the magnet, the desire for peace.

Ambivalence

The desire for peace is purely emotional – a felt need. From a strictly rational perspective, we are also interested in having our preferred solutions accepted by our adversary – getting our way. The emotional and rational concerns must be compromised. We can seldom fully have both peace in the relationship and our preferred solution. The tension between these two desires is illustrated in the Conflict Ambivalence Grid* (see Figure 3 on next page).

---

* Various two-dimensional grid models in conflict behavioral style analysis have been presented by Robert Blake and Jane Mouton, Alan Filley, Kenneth Thomas, and others.

Figure 3: *Conflict Ambivalence Grid*

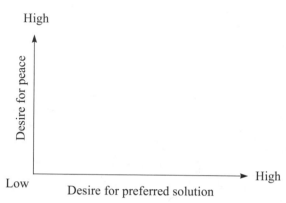

Hard and Soft Bargainers

In attempting to reconcile this ambivalence, each partner strikes an often uneasy balance between the two desires. Some of us care more strongly for one outcome than for the other. The relative strengths of these two desires determines how "hard" we are as bargainers.

The greater our desire for peace, the more likely we are to offer or welcome conciliatory gestures. We may offer concessions on our preferred solution to the issue in dispute. If our desire for peace is low, then we are willing to sacrifice peacefulness in the relationship in order to maximize attainment of our preferred solution.

A person whose balance of desires is like that portrayed by Figure 4 (next page) would be experienced by her Other as a "hard bargainer." In contrast a person whose balance of concerns resembles that in Figure 5 will sacrifice self-interest on substantive issues in order to maintain peaceful relations.

Figure 4: *Conflict Ambivalence Grid*
(Hard bargainer)

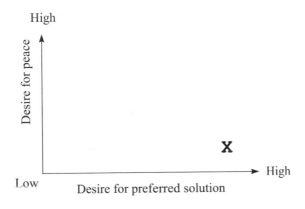

Figure 5: *Conflict Ambivalence Grid*
(Soft bargainer)

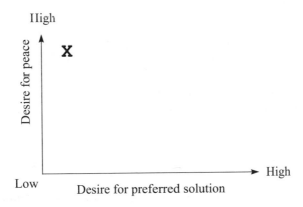

We differ from each other on how we characteristically balance these two desires. And, the balances we strike may vary from situation to situation. Still, in any conflict, each of us is concerned about both keeping the relationship harmonious and getting what we want from preferred solutions to the substantive issues. To the extent that desire for peace exists at all, it is a force toward conciliation.

Catharsis

Sigmund Freud was the most notable, but not the first, to advocate "the talking cure." He rediscovered what all of us experience from time to time in our daily lives: Simply talking about our troubles relaxes physical and emotional tension. "Supportive counseling" is little more than the talking cure packaged as weekly appointments with an empathetic listener. Counseling provides a regular opportunity for people to talk about their worries and problems with a good sounding board. This discharge of pent-up tension is called "catharsis."

Direct Engagement

How does catharsis help resolve interpersonal conflicts? No doubt you have discovered that when you are in conflict with someone, you can discharge some of the anger and tension by expressing it in ways other than direct face-to-face talking. Maybe you go to the gym for a vigorous game of squash, or you slam doors, or you talk to a friend. These are ways to drain off the overflow tension created by conflict.

But the long-term value of simply releasing angry energy indirectly is limited. In these examples, it is not discharged in the presence of the person who is the object of your anger. Therefore, you do not have the satisfaction of "direct engagement," of expressing your anger directly toward its object. Rather, you are expressing it only toward a symbol of the object – the squash ball, the door, the mental image of your foe as you talk with the friend. By engaging only with the symbol of your Other, you are denied:

- The primal satisfaction of striking out (verbally, of course) against your foe, and
- The opportunity to hear and respond to your Other's responses and reactions that can lead to an exchange of conciliatory gestures.

Catharsis resulting simply from aggression toward a symbolic target provides a temporary release of tension. So, catharsis resulting from aggression displaced onto a symbol can help dissipate stress that is spawned by conflict. But catharsis during real-time Dialogue with your Other also releases tension. More importantly, it occurs in a setting where conciliatory gestures can be responded to by either of you as they arise in conversation.

Recalling our discussion in the chapter "Skills for Dialogue," we should recognize that catharsis results from effective assertiveness just as is does from aggression – without the risk of escalation or spiraling up that happens when we act out aggressively. So, while we acknowledge the value of catharsis, we also prefer that it occurs via assertiveness.

So a caution is in order. Catharsis via aggression carries risk. Psychological research shows that face-to-face verbal aggression can deepen conflict if done in an inappropriate context. Self Mediation, particularly the Cardinal Rules that outlaw Walk-aways and Power-plays throughout a Dialogue, provides some insurance against harmful effects of catharsis via aggression.

Inhibitory Reflex in Territorial Behavior

Scientists who study the social behavior of animals in their natural habitats – ethologists – have observed a pair of instincts that consistently control the behavior of two adult members of the same species during territorial encounters.

Aggression

The first instinct is aggression. Aggression occurs every time an animal perceives that another is violating a territorial boundary, or appears to have that intention. When a territorial violation occurs, the "home-turf" animal rushes to meet the intruder with threatening postures, and may physically attack unless the intruder immediately withdraws. Most conflicts between animals are resolved in this way – one individual retreats. It is this retreat from encounter that in modern human behavior we have labeled the Wrong Reflex #1: Distancing.

Sometimes, the intruder persists in attempting to take possession of the home-turf animal's territory. Then a fight occurs. But fights between animals in the wild hardly ever result in death. Why not? Because a second instinct prevents violence from escalating beyond an safe level, and serves as a mechanism for peaceful resolution.

This second instinct is the inhibitory reflex. We all have seen the inhibitory reflex happen, without paying much attention to it. Consider this backyard scenario: Two dogs, "Rex" and "Tiny," get into a territorial fight in one's yard. Tiny quickly recognizes the futility of fighting with the stronger Rex and rolls over, showing his soft belly. Rex, if he chose, could bite Tiny's belly and possibly kill him. But by rolling over (a conciliatory gesture), Tiny has elicited the inhibitory reflex in Rex. Rex is utterly constrained by instinct from biting Tiny's tummy. Any sign of self-protective posturing by Tiny would release Rex from the inhibitory reflex's constraining muzzle, freeing him to bite.

So the picture is this: Tiny lies belly-up on the ground, his soft, vulnerable tummy exposed, whimpering nervously. Meanwhile, Rex is poised with perilous fangs hovering above the submissive Tiny, growling menacingly. This scene continues a few moments, long enough for Rex to drive home his point that he is the winner. Rex then struts slowly away, the proud victor.

Tiny's conciliatory gesture automatically triggered Rex's inhibitory reflex, preventing dangerous escalation of the conflict. Where did Tiny's conciliatory gesture come from? Certainly Tiny could predict that to continue fighting would have dire consequences to his health. He probably knew it was an uphill battle before ever encountering Rex to start with. He is not blind; he could see Rex's superior size and strength. So why did Tiny get involved in this hopeless encounter?

Tiny and Rex have dog-versions of what we have called in this book emotional issues. Tiny made a show of confronting Rex because his self-esteem, his pride, required it. But Tiny is no fool. He did so "knowing" instinctively that he could trust Rex to inhibit his aggression as soon as he employed the conciliatory gesture trick. Tiny got his "day in court" with Rex without getting hurt. So, dogs and other animals are instinctively equipped with the "knowledge" of how to use the conciliatory gesture whenever it is needed to elicit the inhibitory reflex in others.

Among dogs, as well as in every other species of predatory social animal on earth, the conciliatory gesture automatically elicits the inhibitory reflex. This happens just as surely as the aggressive reflex is triggered when an intruder enters another's territory. So aggression and its inhibition are the two instincts that control intraspecies fights.

Inhibition in Humans

Now, what about us humans? We are not driven by instinct as absolutely as are animals. Still, we have evolved from common ancestors with other animals who share our planet today, and so we share an evolutionary heritage. We are different from animals in many ways; we are also similar to animals in some remarkable ways. The fact that the aggression and inhibitory reflexes are found throughout the animal world offers us an opportunity to learn something about how we handle human conflict by examining conflict between animals.

Before looking at how people follow a similar pattern in two-person conflicts, let's mention some differences between humans and animals that must be considered in drawing any parallels:

1) Having developed spoken language, we usually conduct our aggression – forays into enemy territory – via words rather than by physical attacks and attack posturing.
2) Our "territory" is often less concrete and geographical in nature, and more abstract and conceptual. Intruders in our homes and our offices, of course, arouse home-turf protective reactions. But so do co-workers who attempt to take over part of our job responsibilities, employees who overstep the bounds of their authority, spouses who attempt to

impose a sex-role stereotype on their partners, colleagues who do not acknowledge the privileges of our professional rank, and salespeople who insist on taking up our time. In these examples, our "territory" is not clearly delineated. These uncertain boundaries make it difficult to determine whether a trespass is accidental or intentional.

3) In most human disputes, both participants often feel that they are on their own home turf and are simply protecting themselves from unwarranted intrusion by the Other. So it is much less clear that one individual is "in the wrong" by knowingly violating boundaries. More often, both participants feel their rights are violated by the other.

4) We have more free will in controlling how we behave than do animals. That is, we can choose to act differently from how our emotions propel us to act.

5) We live our daily lives in unnaturally large groups such as cities and megacorporations, requiring us to interact closely with people whom we do not know well enough to trust.

Natural Weapons

One additional difference between humans and animals is a key to understanding two-person conflicts: People do not have "natural weapons." Natural weapons, like sharp claws and long teeth, are parts of the body that could do physical damage to another in a physical fight. Every other predatory social animal has natural weapons – humans do not. We do, however, have vestiges of natural weapons, such as finger- and toe-nails and the "canine" teeth. These features of our bodies are puny remnants of what used to be, earlier in our evolutionary history, effective natural weapons that were used for preying on other animals for food and for sorting out the dominance hierarchy (the "pecking order") in our social groups. Over the past few million years, however, these body parts have become less useful and have physically diminished.

What purpose does the inhibitory reflex serve for animals? Why did it evolve in the first place? Clearly, if Tiny's conciliatory gesture did not cause Rex to back off, Rex could use his long sharp teeth and powerful jaws to kill Tiny – not as prey for food, but as a member of the same species with whom he is simply sorting out dominance. If the natural weapons that animals have for predation and food-acquisition were used without restraint, then the species would be less effective in reproducing and succeeding in its environment. The inhibitory reflex evolved in parallel with natural weapons as a behavioral mechanism to restrain their destructive use within social groups. So the combination of the aggressive impulse to perceived territorial intrusion, along with the inhibitory reflex, serves as a very effective behavioral mechanism in maintaining social order among animals.

Our Unreliable Inhibitory Reflex

Now let's look again at humans. As our natural weapons have become vestigial over the past several million years, the inhibitory reflex which had previously evolved to accompany them has also become vestigial. So, our inhibitory reflex is far weaker and less reliable than that of non-human animals. This would not present a problem except that over the past few thousand years (far too short a time for evolution to have produced adaptive changes) we have drastically changed the structure of social and community life. In early human social groupings, dominance had to be sorted out only in well-structured groups of a couple of dozen members, all of whom were born and reared together. When the group became larger than twenty or so, several members split off to form another group.

Today we live and work in "unnatural" social groupings. Organizations force people into ongoing, interdependent relationships. But co-workers did not grow up together and therefore did not learn at an early age to accept a position in the dominance hierarchy. Organizations are usually larger than the naturally occurring groups we evolved in, and for which our social behavioral mechanisms are adapted. Even the modern marriage may be an arrangement that is imposed on us by the demands of our exceedingly complex communities. Certainly the equal-status, shared-power marriage is a recent social invention that is more congruent with twentieth-century humanistic values than with social values of previous millennia.

Predicament of Modern Life

So now, on the threshold of the third millennium, we humans find ourselves in ongoing interdependent relationships that we are not well-equipped through evolution to manage peacefully. Specifically, the threats to our "turf" at work and at home arouse our self-defensive aggressive reflex, yet we do not have a reliable behavioral mechanism to extricate ourselves from the retaliatory cycle once it begins. Using a conciliatory gesture no longer ensures an automatic inhibitory reflex from our Other. Since our conflicts normally take the form of verbal arguments, verbal conciliatory gestures are often not noticed, or are misinterpreted as deceptive, manipulative tactics. Even when a conciliatory gesture is heard, it can be taken as an opportunity to "go for the jugular" and win the fight.

The human inhibitory reflex is weak. But it does exist, and the modest automatic impulse that remains can be exploited as the critically important fourth force for bringing harmony to two-person conflicts. It is the element in Self Mediation that triggers the Breakthrough, permitting the negotiation of both-gain agreements. It is that gentle nudge to respond in kind when one says to us, "I'm sorry" or "I made a mistake."

Harmonizing the Forces

Fatigue from sustained effort, desire for peaceful relationships, release of tension through catharsis, and the inhibitory reflex to conciliatory gestures are human experiences that are not limited only to Self Mediation. They occur constantly through daily living. The power of Self Mediation for managing differences lies in the harnessing of these forces to bring harmony to discordant relationships. The structure, context, rules, and tasks prescribed by this four-step method help these four psychological dynamics join together in producing that special window of opportunity for interpersonal peace – the Breakthrough.

Chapter 20:

A SUMMARY:
HOW SELF MEDIATION TURNS
CONFLICT INTO COOPERATION

Finally, standing upon the behavioral science foundation laid in the previous two chapters, let's review Self Mediation, summarizing how each step contributes to transforming conflict into cooperation, making interpersonal peace.

Step 1: FIND A TIME TO TALK

Setting a time and the groundrules for a conversation with your Other about the issues that concern you . . .

- Establishes communication, the most fundamental and essential requirement for interpersonal peace.
- Establishes Cardinal Rule #1, which prevents the Wrong Reflex of Distancing from blocking resolution by ensuring that both participants are present and actively involved.
- Establishes Cardinal Rule #2, which prevents the Wrong Reflex of Coercion from resulting in defeat of one participant, laying the basis for future deterioration of the relationship.

Step 2: PLAN THE CONTEXT

Preparing the time-and-place environment for your talk . . .
- Ensures steady progress through the confrontation phase of the Dialogue, ensuring that both participants complete the "journey to the top of the mountain."
- Ensures sufficient time for catharsis to occur during the confrontation phase so that genuine conciliatory gestures can emerge.
- Protects the Dialogue from the interruptions and distractions that can cause your meeting to fail.

Step 3: TALK IT OUT

The Opening . . .
- Establishes a climate of non-defensiveness and optimism.
- Reaffirms commitment to the Cardinal Rules of engagement during the Dialogue.
- Establishes an expectation that a both-gain solution will be found through joint searching.

The Invitation launches the Dialogue.

The Dialogue empowers the initiator of this Method to guide communication with the Other to a constructive conclusion by performing . . .
- Task #1: Staying engaged in the Essential Process, keeping participants in uninterrupted contact long enough for the four psychological forces to combine to produce conciliatory gestures; and
- Task #2: Supporting the Other's conciliatory gestures, so that friendly comments will not be taken as opportunities to "score a point in the win-lose game" thereby sabotaging progress; leading to . . .

The <u>Breakthrough</u>, in which both partners' attitudes shift from me-against-you to us-against-the-problem, a window of opportunity during which they can . . .

Step 4: MAKE A DEAL

Once Breakthrough occurs, framing a behaviorally specific agreement . . .

- Allows joint consent to decisions that require consensus.
- Creates a mutually acceptable plan for activities that require participation by both partners.
- Ensures a balanced give-and-take that provides an incentive for each participant to fulfill his/her obligations in the agreement.
- Enhances interpersonal trust.
- Provides an experience in successfully getting around the "boulder in the road," increasing participants' optimism about their ability to manage their differences and resolve disputed issues in the future.

Part 6

COMMON COURTESY

Chapter 21:

BETTER LIVING
THROUGH MEDIATION IN EVERYDAY LIFE:
THREE EPIPHANIES

Taking no credit for carefully planning the trip, I have meandered along a career path that has led me past some meaningful milestones. Two have changed my course in years past. A third occurs today as I prepare *Managing Differences* for its second edition.

For over 25 years I have devoted my professional life to designing, refining, practicing, and teaching communication tools that harness the power of mediation. Each milestone has marked another epiphany, revealing an even simpler tool. Each successive simplification makes the magic of mediation ever more accessible to people as they manage their differences everyday in their ongoing interdependent relationships. Let me share the three epiphanies.

Communication tool #1: *Simple Mediation*

My study of conflict and ways to resolve it began early in graduate school. Some years later, while teaching organizational behavior at the University of Hartford in 1979, a career-changing insight flashed before my mind's eye:

> *Mediation does not require*
> *a professionally trained mediator.*

Looking back from today's perspective, this doesn't seem particularly profound. But in the climate of the times, it seemed a lapse of common sense.

Reflecting on my errors as a fledgling mediator-consultant, I came to realize that mediation can be simplified so that people without extensive training can tap the subtle power of this tool for interpersonal peacemaking.

The Need in Organizations

This fact is particularly relevant to organizations. Supervisors and managers serve on the front line in the daily assault waged by conflict against the bulwarks defending their firm's performance and profitability. Simple Mediation (called "Managerial Mediation" in this context) is a potent weapon in their defensive arsenal. The ability to resolve disputes between employees is an increasingly important competency as organizational hierarchies become flatter, which in turn causes staff to become more interdependent.

The insight that managers can mediate was captured in an article published in 1982*, and has evolved into the core content of a one-day management training program, "The Manager-as-Mediator Seminar."

The notion that managers can mediate was provocative, as well as novel. My early advocacy of Managerial Mediation in presentations to fellow dispute resolvers sparked controversy. These were audiences who generally regarded the practice of mediation as the private preserve of "professional mediators." In those early days, mediation was an emerging area of professional practice, venturing beyond its classical role in labor relations. Doing mediation was widely assumed to require extensive preparatory training and lofty credentials. Mediation was regarded as a nascent field of professional practice, just as medicine, law, psychology, and social work had once been.

In counterpoint, my presentations to conferences of colleagues contended that the essence of mediation is simply good management. That is, encouraging dialogue, managing the context of discussions, promoting non-adversarial search for consensus, and defining agreement in behavioral terms are simply good ways to solve workplace problems.

I eagerly concede that the *commercial* practice of mediation should be regulated to assure consumers of the competency of their mediators, just as other fields of commercial practice – medicine, law, and accountancy, for example – are regulated. Surely, just being well-versed in health care does not warrant hanging out a shingle as a medical doctor. Licensure, certification, and other regulatory requirements for the practice

* D. Dana, Mediating interpersonal conflict in organizations: Minimal conditions for resolution, *Leadership and Organization Development Journal,* Volume 3, Number 1, 1982.

of professional specialties are needed to protect consumers against harm by malpractice. Regulation is especially important for the practice of invasive services, where the consumer is most vulnerable.

But recall from chapter 16 that in Simple Mediation, the third party plays a quite passive role, not an invasive one. Consequently, although it is not as powerful as intervention by a professionally qualified mediator, Simple Mediation is a valuable form of "self-help" that does not subject parties to risk. It merely outlines a way to have a conversation about a problem.

So I advocated to the field of dispute resolution that this communication tool be made widely available, just as we avail the public of medical information to support their self-healthcare. I am gratified that Managerial Mediation is now widely acknowledged as a critical competency for supervisors. Indeed, mediation is included in the curricula of a growing number of graduate schools of business in the United States and internationally.

Communication tool #2: *Self Mediation*

Let's fast-forward to 1988 for the next epiphany:

Mediation does not require a third party.

Recall that the core content of the first edition of *Managing Differences* was termed "The 4-Step Method" – the same communication tool that is now called Self Mediation in the third edition. Reviewer comments on the tool were favorable, particularly those from fellow mediators. The concept plainly made sense. But had I declared from the start that "mediation does not require a third party," my colleagues would surely have been concerned that I had taken leave of my senses.

After all, what is more definitive of "mediation" than the involvement of a third party?

But it was self-evident that no amount of proselytizing about Simple Mediation could, nor should, result in third parties being involved in *all* interpersonal disputes. The vast majority of day-to-day conflicts will continue to be handled by the people who are personally involved, without third party help. Indeed, I would be concerned about a decline in self-responsibility if we ran to a mediator each time a Clash erupted.

Does this mean that everyday disputes are left to founder on the shoals of our differentness, untrained helmsmen at the wheel? Fortunately not. Simple Mediation can be even further simplified so that *everyone* can use it as a self-help communication tool – "Self Mediation." As this book has described, the essential functions of a third-party mediator are integrated into the role of one person in the dispute – the one who proactively chooses to initiate a Dialogue to resolve it. So, the "Self-mediator" wears two hats simultaneously: A **negotiator** serving one's own self-interests, as well as a **mediator** who performs the vital role behaviors of the absent third party, facilitating the process toward consensus.

As organizations have recognized the need for proactivity and empowerment in their workforces, Self Mediation has emerged as the core content of a second one-day training program, "The Self-as-Mediator Seminar."

Communication tool #3: *Common Courtesy*

The simplification of mediation continues. Now, while preparing the second edition of *Managing Differences,* another epiphany grips my attention:

> *Mediation does not even require an "event."*

Now I'm truly at risk of being dismissed as a loose cannon on the quarter-deck of the ship of the profession! But maybe if I don't define Common Courtesy as any manner of mediation, I will be spared the fate of being thrown overboard into the sea of apostasy. No, I choose to declare from the pulpit of this book that the same underlying psychology that makes Simple Mediation effective, and that makes Self Mediation effective, can be harnessed and put to work in all our daily interactions with the important people in our lives.

Mediation may be thought of as a toolbox containing an assortment of devices for non-adversarial communication about divisive issues. Many well-known tools have been designed for special purposes, ranging from negotiation of international treaties, to labor contract dispute settlement, to divorce mediation. Might we also design a tool to use "on line" every day, in all our interactions with others, to *prevent* conflict? Might there be a tool that can become "second nature" to us, one that just makes our relationships work better?

A visiting lecturer once remarked during my early graduate school days in psychology: "Psychotherapy is too good to be done only with sick people." Might the same be said about mediation? Might the principles of mediation be used as a way of life, not just as a procedure for a mediation event?

"On line" Skills

Indeed, all of us use skills for managing differences "on line," while we interact with others minute-by-minute, unaware that we are doing so. They have been developed throughout life as we learn how to get along with others. We generally don't collect those skills under one umbrella and define them as a "tool." I may be in a minority, but am not unique, as one who has virtually eliminated destructive conflict from my life, although I may be more conscious of how to accomplish this than most.

So it is possible to tame the beast of conflict, gaining mastery over it, preventing the carnage inflicted when it rages out of control. Today's epiphany inspires me to construct such a tool so others can carry it in their toolboxes.

What will such a tool look like? What kind of communication tool can enable us to manage our differences so well that conflict does not arise in the first place? That Blips do not escalate into Clashes? That the Essential Process is a constant feature of communication, not just the focus of special problem-solving meetings? That the Wrong Reflexes do not sabotage daily dialogues?

For now let's call that communication tool "Common Courtesy" – a better term may come along later. No training program to teach Common Courtesy is yet developed. How should such a program be named? "Preventing Conflict" would be a descriptive title. Or, since well-managed differences produce satisfaction and success in our relationships, which are key to a happy life, maybe "Working, Living, and Loving Well"

would not be too ambitious a title. We'll see where the path
leads.

Let's recall the spirit, if not the poetry, of John Lennon's
song, "Imagine." Imagine that, in all interactions in our ongoing,
interdependent relationships, no one used the Wrong Reflexes.
Imagine that no one distanced, disconnected, avoided, withdrew,
or walked away. Imagine that no one coerced, pressured,
intimidated, threatened, or "power-played." Imagine that no one
acted passive-aggressively, using hit-and-run tactics of guerrilla
warfare on the interpersonal battlefield.

Idealistic? Certainly. Utopian? Perhaps. Clearly,
behaving in these ways requires a commitment of time and
energy that may not be practical in relationships in which
interdependency is low – we can simply hang up on an offensive
telephone solicitor. But what about our spouses and children,
our managers and close co-workers, our next door neighbors, our
business partners and key associates? Would not this imagined
behavior prevent decay of workplace teamwork and erosion of
friendships? Would it not prevent the chilling of warm family
love until only the cinder of "cold peace" remains? You and I
imagine that it would.

Choice

So why don't we do it? Why don't we "do the right
thing?" Why don't we routinely join our Others in a spirit of us-
against-the-problem on issues that *must* be resolved to mutual
satisfaction if our relationship is to thrive?

Reviewing my own failings, and observing those of
others, I conclude that we lack *courage*. It is simply safer to
Distance and Coerce than to Dialogue. It is easier to Walk-away
and Power-play than to Talk It Out. Our vulnerabilities are

protected when we avoid, evade, and ignore. Our weaknesses remain hidden when we bluster and intimidate and threaten. The illusion of our faultlessness is preserved when we deny our own hand in the creation of Clashes. Our emotional needs are exposed when we bravely encounter Others in search of common ground. Yes, we *risk* when we act responsibly, electing not to act out our defensiveness. Facing that risk requires courage.

But *we can choose* to act responsibly. We can choose to behave in the best interest of the relationship, instead of in our personal (short-term) self-interest at the expense of the (long term) relationship. The option of acting responsibly, and in our own *enlightened* self-interest, is always available to us. Although the behaviors required to exercise this option are *simple* to understand, but they are not *easy* to perform. They are more the psychological equivalent of high school algebra than of rocket science. It just requires making the courageous choice to act with Common Courtesy.

The Common Courtesies

A full treatment of this choice and the obstacles to making it are perhaps the subject of a future book*. For now, it must suffice to only define two simple "rules of interpersonal engagement" that flow directly from foregoing chapters.

---

* A later formulation of this concept is described as "preventive mediation" in chapter 7 of *Conflict Resolution: Mediation Tools for Everyday Worklife* (McGraw-Hill, 2001). The primary tasks of Preventive Mediation are:
1) Don't walk away
2) Don't power-play
3) Take risks – that is, offer conciliatory gestures
4) Don't exploit others' risks – that is, don't rebuff others' conciliatory gestures

Common Courtesy #1: *I will engage.*
  I will not distance from you emotionally or physically. I
  will join with you in talking out all issues on which we
  must concur to enable either of us to go forward with
  decisions or actions that affect the other. I will join you
  in conversations that you feel are important, even if I do
  not. I will not use distancing from you as retaliation
  when I feel that you have distanced from me. I will
  engage with you, as I ask you to engage with me.

Common Courtesy #2: *I will respect your sovereignty.*
  I will recognize you as the legitimate sovereign reigning
  over your domain. Your rights as a self-determining
  person constitute that domain: The right to express
  yourself; the right to define your own interests, views
  and needs; the right to expect me to listen to you and try
  to understand; the right to have the impact of my actions
  on you considered before I act. I will acknowledge you
  as the unchallenged expert about your experience within
  your sovereign space – you know your thoughts,
  feelings, needs, wants, fears, and aspirations better than
  I, so I will not "should" on you. I will respect your
  sovereignty, as I ask you to respect mine.

Where to Apply the Common Courtesies

Various examples of workplace and family occasions
where we might apply the Common Courtesies could be
discussed as illustrations.

The case of the "tough boss" is familiar to most readers.
You know the type: The boss who seems to enjoy wielding his
power, throwing her political weight around, wearing his
authority like a badge of privilege, dominating her employees
just because she can. Usually unknown to themselves, such

bosses (and their organizations) pay a stiff price for such short-sighted self-indulgence. But in the Darwinian marketplace, these dinosaurs are in decline. The managers who will adapt and survive are those who serve as coaches, resources, facilitators, and mentors to their employees. The future belongs to managers who use Common Courtesy, and to organizations that promote a corporate culture in which the Common Courtesies are the norm.

But I choose to end this chapter, and this book, with an application that is close to my own heart.

Despite the campaign of Dr. Benjamin Spock and his successors over the past half-century to encourage adult society to respect the rights of children, the parental paradigm in western cultures remains largely one of parenthood-as-power. As parents, we unquestioningly accept the "fact" that, because we are the adults in our parent-child partnerships, we have the right to coerce our children to abide our wishes. It is as if Machiavelli's political philosophy should pertain also to our families – "might makes right." Of course, we are devoted custodians of our children. We love them, nurture them, reward their achievements, and encourage their ambitions. But when wills clash, parents often resort to declaring, "Because I'm the mom/dad, that's why!"

Some readers will ask, "So what's wrong with that?" Yes, children need boundaries to be set around socially acceptable behavior. They need protection against the natural consequences of their own dangerous actions. They need their parents to serve as positive role models of adults who have power. But power is not equivalent to exercising self-serving control in violation of the child's sovereignty within her legitimate domain.

I will forego arguing at length the case that parental coercion is bad for the child, bad for the parent, and bad for

society. But briefly note that child abuse – that not-rare-enough
violence by parents against children – is only the most notorious
consequence of extreme parental coercion: Most child abusers
were themselves once abused children. The rage and indignation
that originated in their own experience of being abused
overwhelms their moral sense of right-and-wrong, and they
commit violence against their own children.

But what about the more commonplace struggles by
many more adults (who also once were children) to overcome
their fears of inadequacy, or to contain their senseless
competitiveness? What about those adults whose childhood
experience was marked by "normal" powerlessness –
disempowered by their youth, their smaller size and lesser
strength, their ignorance about the world, their abject
dependency? What about those adults who don't feel equipped
by their "normal" childhoods to handle the rigors of adulthood,
just as the ex-convict doesn't feel equipped to handle life on the
outside after years of being deprived of sovereignty over his
daily existence?

Yes, they survived. They learned to hide in the dark
corners of their privacy to avoid having their sovereignty
usurped by their parents. Did they learn to feel secure in their
personal domains, capable of taking full responsibility for
themselves as autonomous yet socially-responsible adults: As
employees, as bosses, as teammates, as members of communities
and of families? Did they acquire the strength to carry their
share of the load when their relationships become burdened with
responsibility? Did they learn to feel safe enough to trust
enough to be vulnerable enough to love and to be loved?

Too often the answer is no. These, I believe, are the
more subtle costs of parental coercion, even as it is kindly and
gently practiced the way society thinks is normal, acceptable,

and proper – as the parenthood-as-power paradigm dictates. Each generation pays the price; society pays the price.

How can parents, who might like to consider adopting an alternative paradigm, apply the Common Courtesies with their children? How can we rethink our role so that parental Power-plays are disallowed without abandoning our responsibilities as guides and protectors of our children? Is there a practical alternative to parental Power-plays to respond to our children when their actions are inappropriate?

Many positive resources are available in your local bookstore and on the Internet. To supplement these worthy resources, I offer this brief introduction to Common Courtesy as a tentative guide for participating in our partnerships with our children. I intend to explore this new communication tool – the ultimate simplification of mediation – in future research and writing.

Whereof do I speak about parenting? My daughter was born in 1973. I have done my modest best over the years to apply my accruing learnings about mediation and "how to build better relationships" to our father-daughter partnership – learnings now taking shape as the Common Courtesies. Indeed, much of that learning has come to me through her intrinsic wisdom. Without embarrassing Susan by reporting details in this book, and without taking undue credit for the result, I will simply say that I am immensely pleased with the person she is and is becoming, and am proud to be her friend.

That pleasure and pride is surpassed only as I observe Susan's parenting of Seamus Dana Connor and Claribel Zia Connor. Ignoring the considerable risk of grandfatherly bias, I think I see generational inheritance in action. If so, I could wish for no greater legacy – unless you, dear reader, were to observe similar effects in your own progeny, years hence.

Appendix

Appendix 1:

NOTES FOR THE OTHER

I am asking you to join with me in searching for mutually acceptable solutions to certain issues that we disagree about, and work with me to build a better relationship between us.

This process – called "Self Mediation" – requires that we find a time to talk without interruption until we are able to find some agreement. In order for this discussion to be successful, both of us must accept two "Cardinal Rules."

Cardinal Rule #1: *No "Walk-aways"*
    This means we will not walk out, give up, or stop trying until some kind of agreement is reached. Let's agree to accept feeling frustrated and angry during our talk, if necessary, and to persevere even if we want to quit.

Cardinal Rule #2: *No "Power-plays"*
    This means that neither of us will try to impose a one-sided solution. Any solution that involves either of us being coerced to accept the other's demands is not acceptable. We must continue to search for a solution to which we both can agree and from which we both can gain.

If the subject of our dispute involves a decision to which we both must consent, or an activity in which we both must participate, we must reach an agreement. Good agreements are:

- *Behaviorally specific*, meaning that we will discuss in detail WHO, is to do WHAT, by WHEN, for HOW LONG, under what CONDITIONS, etc.
- *Balanced*, so that the agreement is fair for both of us.
- *Written*, to help us remember the details of our agreement in the future.

Thanks for caring enough about our relationship to work with me on this.

(From Managing Differences: How to Build Better Relationships at Work and Home *by Daniel Dana, MTI Publications, 5700 West 79th Street, Prairie Village, Kansas 66208-4604. This appendix may be reproduced without restriction.)*

Appendix 2:

HOW TO USE THIS BOOK
FOR QUICK REFERENCE

This book may look like many others, to be read from start to finish, then to be put on your bookshelf to gather dust.

But this is designed so you can use it as a reference book, more like a dictionary, road atlas, or cookbook. First, read it through once, cover to cover, to familiarize yourself with Self Mediation and how it works. Then keep this with your other reference books – on your desk at work or on the coffee table at home.

Everyone encounters a conflict from time to time in important relationships. Each time you do, reach for this resource. After you have read it once, here is how to use this book:

1) Refresh your understanding of Self Mediation by reviewing Chapter 6: A Skeleton View.

2) Ask yourself this question:
   "Do I feel comfortable using Self Mediation to resolve this conflict?"

3) If you answer yes, go to step 4 below. If you answer no, look through the following possible concerns to more clearly identify the reasons for your discomfort:

   - *I'm not sure it will work.*
   - *I don't know if the Other will do it.*
   - *I feel awkward suggesting we have a meeting.*
   - *I don't want to be the one who initiates it. It would seem like I'm giving in.*
   - *I can't trust the other person to not use unfair power advantage. I am too vulnerable to being punished.*
   - *The conflict/relationship/issue is not important enough to me to go through the trouble and discomfort of talking about it.*
   - *I think my conflict is more of a crisis than Self Mediation is designed to deal with.*
   - *I might get too nervous to do it right.*
   - *I'm concerned that the Other is not strong enough.*
   - *I don't have the time to deal with it.*
   - *I don't want the Other to get upset.*
   - *It's easier just to keep things the way they are now.*
   - *I don't think the Other would understand what to do.*
   - *I'm afraid I would just give in to the Other's pressure.*
   - *I would get too angry.*
   - *I know the Other will not change; it would just be wasted effort.*

Your concerns probably fall into any of five categories. Review the suggested sections of the book to explore your questions:

A) Concerns about importance of the problem. See Chapter 1.
B) Concerns about appropriateness of the problem. See Chapters 5 and 15.
C) Concerns about whether Self Mediation can solve the problem. See Chapters 14 and 15, and Part 5.
D) Concerns about yourself (confidence in your ability to use the method). See Chapters 10 and 11.
E) Concerns about your Other's ability or willingness to participate in Self Mediation. See Chapters 8 and 15.

4) Answer this question:
"After reviewing the relevant information in this book, am I confident that Self Mediation is designed to resolve conflicts of the kind I am concerned with?"

(Note: Do not expect yourself to be entirely free of apprehension. Review the discussion about discomfort in Chapter 13 if you are tempted to avoid a Dialogue with your Other as Self Mediation prescribes.)

5) If your answer is yes, do it. Use the checklist on the next page to be sure you're fully prepared. If your answer is no, look at alternative recommendations in chapters 5 and 15.

6) Congratulate yourself for being a problem-solver, not a problem-avoider!

CHECKLIST

Before Step 1 ("Find a Time to Talk"),

☐ Review "How to Use This Book for Quick Reference" (Appendix 2) to be sure the solution fits the problem.

☐ Review Self Mediation (chapter 6).

☐ Prepare the wording of a clear, concise, and objective statement of the issue to be talked about.

Before Step 3 ("Talk It Out"), be sure you've covered the following:

☐ Both schedules cleared for adequate time period?

☐ Interruptions prevented? (phone or walk-ins)

☐ No distractions? (seating comfort, visual movement, sound, thirst, temperature, etc.)

☐ Both agree to stay until agreement is reached?

☐ Both agree to no Walk-aways (Cardinal Rule #1)?

☐ Both agree to no Power-Plays (Cardinal Rule #2)?

☐ Do you have the Essential Process clearly in mind?

Appendix 3:

TALES OF SUCCESS

Since first appearing in 1989, *Managing Differences* has been used as a sourcebook for corporate training programs and continuing education seminars and as a textbook for academic courses that have been attended by thousands. Participants are often invited to submit reports of their real-life applications of Self Mediation and of Simple (Managerial) Mediation. Six of their reports are included here so readers of the third edition can see how others have used these communication tools to build better relationships at work and home.

Some details of these cases have been disguised to preserve anonymity of the people involved.

Case #1:

Balancing Work and Family

Richard and I had been married nearly ten years when he decided to quit his job as an assistant branch manager of a bank and go to law school. About the time his school began, my boss was elected to the state house of representatives, which would require his being out of town from January to mid-April for the next two years. I would have to handle his responsibilities as well as my own. On top of everything, I am in the middle of my master's degree program in business, taking two courses each semester.

These changes and stresses threw our marriage into a crisis. Previously, Richard and I had shared the household tasks of cooking, laundry, grocery shopping, and general cleaning about equally. We don't have children, and we had earned similar salaries in our jobs, so it was pretty easy to get things done. We ate out in restaurants some of the time, and we hired a cleaning lady to come in once every two weeks. Looking back, life was so easy then!

Without Richard's income, we had to cut out the restaurants and the cleaning lady. He got in the habit of staying in the den studying through the evening. At first, I felt OK about fixing dinner and cleaning up after, so that he could take only a short break from his studies. But I also had to study for my two classes: Business Economics and Corporate Financial Analysis – pretty demanding courses. When I asked Richard to do more of the household tasks, he objected, saying that doing well in law school was more important than cleaning house. When I reminded him about my school obligations, he dismissed them, saying that "business school is kindergarten compared to law school."

We had hit an impasse. I began to just fix myself an easy snack in the evening and let Richard fend for himself. Sometimes he would come in the kitchen to make a peanut butter sandwich without saying a word. Other times, he would order a pizza or Chinese food, having it delivered to the outside door of the den, and not offer any to me. Things got pretty tense. That spring semester was a time I never want to repeat!

In June I took a class called "Managing Organizational Conflict" taught by Daniel Dana, in which I learned about Self Mediation. Although it was a course in business school, I knew that I could use what I was learning at home just as well.

I decided to ask Richard for time to talk about our impasse. He agreed, despite his study schedule. I have always trusted that Richard is committed to our marriage and is willing to work on it. We decided to fix breakfast together the next Sunday morning and then talk as long as necessary to find some solutions to our work and family balancing act.

Richard described how unfair he felt it was to have to jeopardize his performance in law school to do housework. He claimed that other law students did not have any responsibilities other than school. (I still don't believe that is true. There are lots of married women in law school and I doubt that their husbands do all the housework. But I didn't argue this point with him.) In reply, I described how unfair I felt it is to be burdened with extra duties while I also have school obligations. Besides, it was Richard's decision to quit his job to attend law school – why should I have to sacrifice for that? I recognized these concerns as the emotional issue of "justice," as described in *Managing Differences.*

The Breakthrough happened when Richard revealed that he was feeling afraid that he wasn't smart enough to excel in law school, and that he had made a big mistake by quitting his job to undertake this challenge. When he opened up to me about his fear, I just melted. I expressed my confidence in him and gave him a long, warm hug. He immediately became much more sympathetic to my needs. That was an obvious Breakthrough!

We decided to make a list together of all the household tasks that had to get done. Then we took turns selecting one task that we would do until all had been taken. We also decided to spend *every* Sunday morning together, away from school work. We both now really look forward to Sunday mornings to keep our cooperative spirit going. Today is November 18, and it's still working!

Case #2:

That's Not Your Job!

Janet and I are registered nurses who work the evening shift in a large teaching hospital. Janet is in the Education Division, and I am a Shift Supervisor in the Clinical Division. We must interact often, so we have an "ongoing interdependent relationship."

Several weeks ago Janet began attending shift report meetings at which clinical information about patients is passed along from one shift to the next. Sometimes she would make comments of a clinical nature while patient reports were being given. It thought that it was unnecessary for her to attend, and that it was inappropriate for her to comment on patients that she had not seen. Besides, her job was in Education, not in Clinical.

So, when Janet appeared at the start of a shift report meeting last week, I politely (I thought!) asked her not to attend. She became upset and stormed out of the room. She quit coming to any of the shift report meetings where I was present and began acting cool toward me. And, she took up to thirty minutes to respond to my pages for her. She also failed to notify me of important information about training events. I recognize these behaviors as examples of Wrong Reflex #1: Distancing.

All this happened before I read *Managing Differences.* Since my relationship with Janet was not getting any better on its own, I decided to try Self Mediation.

I approached Janet and told her I wanted to meet with her to discuss the breakdown in our relationship "for the good of the hospital." At first she was reluctant but finally agreed to meet me in a conference room. I began the meeting by thanking her for joining me to "talk it out." I stated my view of the problem as the lack of communication between us that had been going on since I asked her not to attend shift report meetings. Janet responded angrily that I was too protective of my role and that I overreacted whenever she tried to be involved. She also felt that I viewed her role as unimportant and that I didn't like her.

I explained that I felt our roles were different and complementary, but that one is not more important than the other. I also said that her late responses to my pages sometimes made me look bad to people who were waiting for me to get back to them with the information I needed from her. She apologized and said she would be more prompt in the future – a "conciliatory gesture." I immediately thanked her for that commitment.

Janet went on to explain that she was embarrassed by the way I told her I didn't want her to attend shift report meetings, since other people were in the room at the time. I apologized for my bad timing, and explained my reasons. I said that, although she is a registered nurse, she had not seen the patients being reported on. And, I disclosed that there had been some comments from the arriving shift that they saw her input as being more distracting than helpful. Janet said that she understood better "where I was coming from," and suggested that we clarify how our roles should interface – "Breakthrough!"

We made a Deal that Janet would be welcome to attend report meetings as an observer in order to keep her "finger on the pulse" of educational needs of staff in the Clinical Division. She also agreed to send a written memo to me two weeks prior to any planned educational sessions. She also agreed to respond to my pages within ten minutes.

The Deal is working thus far (three weeks after our Dialogue). It is a both-gain solution, since each of us are benefiting. This has been a real eye-opener for me about how simple and easy it is to work out petty misunderstandings that otherwise have negative consequences on our workplace environment, and potentially on patient care.

Case #3:

A Marriage Saved?

Alex and I have been married for six years. I'm a stay-at-home mom of two little ones, and we have pretty traditional values about marriage. During our first year together we communicated fairly well, but we haven't done so well the past few years.

Some history: Sometimes, when I asked Alex to help in the kitchen, he became annoyed and disappears into his den, saying that he has work to do. This didn't seem fair, since I've always helped him when he asked me to. Besides, I didn't really believe he was working in there. I think he was just hiding from me. I was also annoyed when Alex left his coat and shoes lying around as soon as he arrived home from work, after I've spent the day cleaning our home. I didn't understand why we couldn't work as a team around the house. I thought he should take more pride in our home. I also was upset that when I made suggestions to Alex for solutions to simple problems, he felt attacked and got angry.

Alex had received a copy of *Managing Differences* in a training program at work, and I saw it lying on the sofa. One afternoon I sat down and read it, and thought Self Mediation might help us. That evening, I asked him if he had read it, but he said he hadn't had time. I know that Alex has never been interested in subjects like that.

A couple of days later I asked Alex if he would be willing to meet with me to talk about our problems, as the book recommends. At first he didn't want to, but when I offered that he pick the time and place, he agreed. We decided to meet after dinner the following night while our kids were at a party at a neighbor's house. Because he usually avoids arguments with me, it was important that "Walk-aways" be prevented. So I asked him to agree to not walk out of our meeting, even if he got upset. He said he thought he could do that, "just this once."

When we started our "Dialogue," I said that I appreciated his willingness to talk. I said that I understood his discomfort about conversations like this, that he feels like they are fights. I reminded him that the book said that this could only work if we stayed face-to-face until we talked through the problem.

Although I thought our problems were much deeper, I decided to focus our conversation on a pretty non-threatening issue: "How to spend our evening time." I knew that I couldn't start out by telling him about my complaints, so I invited him to start by telling me about his feelings and ideas about the issue. I just acted like an interviewer who didn't have a personal interest in the matter. I asked lots of open ended questions that couldn't be answered by yes or no or other short answers. This got him to share more of himself.

Alex seemed on guard at first, but eventually opened up and said that he felt I was always "nagging" at him, and that he hated to be told what to do. This made me angry because my father used to call my mother a "nag" and I promised myself that I would never do that. Our discussion got pretty heated. Once Alex stood up to walk out, but I reminded him that he promised to stay, so he sat down. He is really uncomfortable with "fights." Finally I broke down and cried. I told Alex how much our marriage meant to me, and that I was afraid of getting divorced.

I guess that made Alex realize how much pain I had been in, and he said he wanted to work things out too. He actually cried too, which I had never seen him do. I recognized this as a "Breakthrough," because we had both made conciliatory gestures that exposed our vulnerability. The shift from you-against-me to us-against-the-problem had taken place, and we were able to work as a team to resolve our problems.

I explained that my "nagging" was just my attempts to be helpful, but I now understand that he felt controlled by me. He explained that he ignored my requests and suggestions in order to maintain his independence. Once we identified this as the problem, I realized that I had had the "Bad Person Illusion" about Alex, thinking that he was lazy and didn't care about our marriage. And he realized that he had the Bad Person Illusion about me as being a nag.

Our "Deal" was pretty simple: I would give him space, and he would pay attention to the things that he knew bothered me about our home. And, we agreed to find some time one evening each week to talk about our annoyances with each other. We hadn't felt so close since the very beginning of our marriage. It's been three months since our first Dialogue, and our relationship is better than ever.

I shudder to think what might have happened if I hadn't found that book on the sofa. It took us over two hours to talk it out; Alex and I had *never* talked that long about a problem before. I'm convinced that if we hadn't starting communicating, our marriage would have been in trouble. We still have problems, but I'm optimistic that, if we keep communicating this way, we'll stay together forever.

Case #4:

Aftermath of Downsizing

I am an Analyst for an insurance company based in Hartford, Connecticut. I work in a small team that reviews work for our Claims staff. Rose is a Consultant on the team. The title of Consultant is more glamorous, and is one job class higher than that of Analyst. Until recently, our team consisted of four Analysts and four Consultants.

Earlier this year, our company went through a major reorganization that reduced the size of our Claims department. The Consultant positions were eliminated and three new Re-inspector Chief positions were created. Rose did not get one of the three new positions, and was moved to an Analyst position.

Rose has been with the company for nearly twenty years, and is very good at what she does. She is outspoken to the point of abrasiveness sometimes, and displays her knowledge and authority at every opportunity. By nature, I am somewhat reserved and generally a rather quiet person.

As a result of the reorganization, I assumed the responsibility of the Catastrophe Coordinator. As the title indicates, this role involves responding to storms, earthquakes, floods, and other natural disasters. The Catastrophe Coordinator works with claim handlers, sets up offices, responds to the news media, and acts as a liaison to our department heads. I viewed being Catastrophe Coordinator as a lot of extra work, but welcomed the new responsibilities. Rose had expressed interest in the position, viewing it as prestigious, and was upset at not receiving the appointment.

Last February a severe ice storm crippled New York. I approached Rose, who had handled storms over the years, to solicit her advice. She was distinctly unhelpful. I knew Rose was a valuable resource. Being new in the position of Catastrophe Coordinator, I really needed her expertise.

I had recently attended a corporate seminar on "How to Resolve Workplace Conflict" in which we learned how to use Self Mediation. *Managing Differences* was included in the package of course materials that each participant received. So, I decided to "talk it out" with Rose.

I asked her if we could talk to clarify our new responsibilities subsequent to the reorganization. I was careful not to imply that she was doing anything wrong; I framed it as "our" problem, not as a criticism of her. Rose did not at first feel it was necessary, but I appealed to her sense of duty to the company, saying, "You and I might have our differences, but we are both employees of [the company] – we are paid well for doing our jobs the best we can. We owe it to [the company] to work together well, don't you agree?" I invited Rose to select a time and place convenient for her. She suggested the next morning at 7:30 in a particular conference room. I usually don't come to work until 8:30 (we work on a flex-time system), but I readily agreed to the time she preferred.

The floodgates opened as soon as we sat down at 7:30. Rose (who is fifteen years older than I) criticized me for being inexperienced and not ready for the responsibilities of Catastrophe Coordinator. I responded that it was indeed a challenge, but that I feel I can learn quickly. Besides, it was someone else, not I, who gave me the assignment. Rose also complained about the new structure, feeling that there will be costly consequences to the company due to the elimination of the Consultant positions. I agreed, and again pointed out that it was not I who made those decisions.

When I read *Managing Differences,* I was intrigued with the idea of acting as a "spearcatcher" to diffuse the other person's anger. So I just let Rose vent her frustrations on me. I suppressed my own pique at being blamed for things that were not my fault, trying not to defensively argue with her. I just tried to ask her questions to let her elaborate on how she felt after the downsizing.

Eventually, Rose expressed her feelings of being lost and no longer an important part of the company. She also revealed her own anxieties about being terminated, and how difficult it would be to get a job at her age. I found myself feeling genuinely sympathetic toward her, understanding her fears of losing her status and her job this late in her career.

I guess I expressed my sympathy effectively so that Rose felt I was not against her. After a while, she said, "How can I help you?" It was a powerful Breakthrough. I took the opportunity to request her help with the immediate crisis of the New York ice storm. I also said that I truly valued her expertise and that I needed "mentoring" by someone with her knowledge of the business. Rose seemed sincerely flattered by my desire to learn from her. We agreed that I could call on her any time I needed for advice on any part of my job.

The "Deal" in Self Mediation is supposed to be balanced and behaviorally specific. My Deal with Rose was not very behaviorally specific, and at first it seemed to be unbalanced in my favor. This concerned me. But I've come to recognize that what Rose gets out of the Deal is affirmation of her knowledge and experience. In fact, she has mentioned to others on our team that she is my "mentor." That's fine with me.

Case #5:

Interdepartmental Conflict

I am an owner and vice president of ODF Industries, a manufacturer of aircraft engine components. In this business, it is imperative that there be strict adherence to the customer's delivery demands.

An unmet delivery was recently brought to my attention and caused me to become involved in a conflict between our manufacturing supervisor, Tom, and our inspection department manager, Miguel. I received a call from a customer inquiring about his order. After discussing the order with our production control manager, I was informed that the order had not been shipped and would probably be delayed several more days.

My brother, who is the Financial Officer of ODF Industries, recently gave me his copy of *Managing Differences*. I was particularly interested in the chapter about "Simple Mediation," which describes how a manager can facilitate dialogue between two employees. The Tom and Miguel conflict seemed to be just the kind of problem that Managerial Mediation is suited for. So I decided to give it a try.

First, I discussed the problem with both Tom and Miguel separately in individual preliminary meetings. It seems that Tom had delivered the order to Miguel for inspection and shipping just in time, but had also delivered two other orders at the same time. Miguel felt that Tom had repeatedly been insensitive to the impact of "bottlenecking" orders into the inspection department at the same time. Miguel felt that Tom was intentionally trying to make his department look bad. Tom vigorously denied doing so, explaining that the manufacturing department just schedules the orders as they come in and can't control the timing any more than Miguel can.

After hearing each manager's side of the story, I explained that I wanted to meet with them together the next day to improve coordination between their departments. I described my role as like that of a "traffic cop" who will help them talk to each other, but will not decide how to solve the problem myself. (This means that I would be acting as a *mediator,* not as an arbitrator. But I didn't use those terms while talking with the two men.) I emphasized that the purpose of the meeting would *not* be to decide who was at fault for the current problem. Instead, our focus would be on planning to prevent future recurrences of the problem.

The "three-way meeting" was held in a neutral office where interruptions could be controlled. After reminding Tom and Miguel of my role as mediator, I asked them to comment on their perceptions of the problem. After a short delay, Tom stated that his responsibility had been completed in a timely manner and that the late delivery was Miguel's fault. Miguel countered that Tom did not acknowledge the unanticipated workload on Miguel's staff caused by Tom's presentation of other equally important jobs. Miguel pointed out that he had numerous, unanticipated demands on his time, whereas Tom was able to direct his problems to other departments. There was a brief silence, and then Tom advised Miguel of several problems and unforeseen circumstances he had dealt with in the past few days. There was a lull in the conversation, and the frustration among the two parties was evident.

After a few moments of silence, Miguel said he realized that Tom's job was one with a lot of responsibility, and he did not mean to imply that Tom's job had less responsibility than his (a "conciliatory gesture"). Then he went on to say that he sometimes felt that Tom acted like he was his boss. Tom started to deny this, but I knew that I had to support Miguel's conciliatory gesture. So I interrupted Tom to ask Miguel to say more about his remark about recognizing the responsibilities in Tom's job. Miguel proceeded to credit Tom with handling a lot of very demanding obligations very capably. Tom responded by saying much the same thing about Miguel. I saw the Breakthrough happening right there before my eyes!

I seized upon this window of opportunity by asking both of them to suggest improvements in how to coordinate the flow of orders between their departments. Without getting too technical in this case report, I'll just say that they worked together as a team to come up with some significant enhancements. I jotted down notes about their ideas as they spoke. I brought the meeting to a close by congratulating Miguel and Tom on the mature and competent way they resolved the problem. I also said that I would have my secretary organize my notes into a memo outlining their ideas and give them each a copy for review and corrections, if needed.

That was over two months ago. I have held three follow-up meetings to troubleshoot their plan, but few problems have arisen. More importantly, the few problems that did surface were quickly fixed in a cooperative spirit.

In summary, my use of Managerial Mediation was a success. It is so simple, but I had never thought to approach problems like this in the past. I was amazed at how easy it was to use, and how effective it was in opening lines of communication and allowing the people involved to develop their own solutions to the problems. I've scheduled a training session to enable all managers and supervisors at ODF Industries to mediate employee conflicts.

Case #6:

But They Said You Said . . . !

I have learned from working for Housing Services at the University that conflict is inevitable. As a Resident Director, I have been witness to or even directly involved with many different conflicts. The conflict I would like to describe for you is one between two Resident Assistants who were responsible for different floors within the same building. Kelly was new, while Rebecca had been a Resident Assistant last year.

Understandably, Kelly tried hard to fit in to the group. Rebecca soon came to me complaining that Kelly was disruptive, untrustworthy, manipulative, and overbearing. It seems two of Rebecca's friends had had classes with Kelly, so Rebecca believed what her friends said. The residents on Rebecca's floor also claimed that Kelly had been making uncomplimentary comments about Rebecca's abilities as a Resident Assistant.

In my position as the supervisor of both, I decided to try Managerial Mediation to settle this conflict. As a psychology major who intends to go to graduate school next year, I had read *Managing Differences* over the summer. Since both women had come to me complaining of problems, I had no difficulty getting them to agree to a meeting. I held a brief preliminary meeting with each one separately mostly to explain my role as a mediator.

To start off the mediation session, I stated that I was pleased that they both wanted to work out this problem. I established the Cardinal Rules by explaining that we must stay until we reach a conclusion (no "Walk-aways") and that we would seek a both-gain solution (no "Power-plays"). We agreed on the importance of confidentiality. I explained once again my role, not as a member of the discussion or a decision-making judge, but rather as a facilitator of the Dialogue between them.

Rebecca started by blaming Kelly for the problems they were having (the "Bad Person Illusion"). Soon both were getting out pent-up feelings and clearing up some misunderstandings and miscommunications. They found they had both been listening to other people and trusting them instead of each other. Also, they realized that the residents had used them against each other to get their way. So quickly it was no longer Rebecca and Kelly against each other, but Rebecca and Kelly against the problem.

They agreed to check out questions about each other's behavior in the future, rather than just assume that what they heard was true. We also agreed to have a ten minute "tune up" meeting each week for the next month. It has now been three months, and Kelly and Rebecca have become friends.

I am so proud that my first attempt at mediating went so well. I am looking forward to future occasions to prove its value.

Appendix 4:

MANAGING CULTURAL DIFFERENCES

Karen likes to spend a half-hour each week privately with each of her employees to sound out their concerns about the office. David, her colleague in another work unit, thinks this practice is not only a waste of time, but also is unwise. "Why take the lid off Pandora's box?" he asks.

Guillermo, 32 years old and married with four children, recently declined a promotion that would have required moving to a city 800 miles away. He explained the he does not want to leave his seven brothers and sisters and their families who live nearby. Luther, who works closely with Guillermo, thinks it is a sign of immaturity that his Hispanic colleague would give up this career opportunity for reasons that he should have grown out of by this age. Luther's respect for Guillermo is reduced one notch.

James, who grew up in an inner-city black neighborhood, is being interviewed for a sales position by Lisa, who is white. Lisa notices that James does not maintain eye contact while listening to her. She forms an immediate impression that James lacks assertiveness, and will probably not be able to handle important clients.

Some facts

The Hudson Institute in its landmark study *Workforce 2000: Work and Workers for the 21ˢᵗ Century* (1987), and again in *Workforce 2020* (1997), has documented the rapid cultural diversification in American workplaces. Considering these facts along with the warp-speed globalization of business, only the most myopic observer could fail to conclude that the days of white male hegemony in the arena of the workplace are over. Workers comprise an increasingly rainbow coalition. The challenge of managing culture-based differences at work is upon us.

In reply to this challenge, "managing cultural diversity" has become one of the hottest topics in the training industry. Many presentations at annual national conferences of the American Society for Training and Development and other human resource professional associations address cross-cultural issues. Consulting firms specializing in helping organizations manage cultural diversity abound.

Facing the challenge

The usual response is to conduct programs designed to raise the awareness of dominant-culture employees about the values and norms of other groups:
- David seems unaware that women tend to focus on relationship issues more than do men.

- Luther seems unaware the Hispanics place a higher value on extended family relationships than do most Anglos.
- Lisa seems unaware that blacks from some subcultures within the United States keep eye contact while speaking but not while listening, the reverse of the pattern typical of majority-culture whites.

Information like this is typically conveyed in cross-cultural training programs for dominant-culture employees. The assumption underlying such "awareness" training is that, after completion of the program, participants are supposed to not only understand minority cultures better, but also to change how they behave toward their members.

But is awareness enough? Does awareness training work?

Reasons for concern

Simply informing members of today's organizations about cultural differences is an incomplete strategy for helping workmates bridge the gaps that impair cooperative work. To achieve maximum benefit, information should be supplemented with behaviorally specific skills or "tools" that equip trainees with practical techniques for solving workplace problems that derive from culture-based differences. Awareness is a first step, but alone is insufficient.

Consider these factors:

1) <u>Resistance to change</u>

Majority-culture trainees may perceive that some personal shortcoming is being "fixed" by the training. Or, they may feel personally blamed for creating the inequities often encountered by minority-culture employees. Or they may perceive, perhaps accurately, that the political power they enjoy as dominant-culture members is in jeopardy of being eroded by cross-cultural training. In short, they perceive that their self-interests are threatened.

When self-interest is threatened, defensiveness is automatically and instinctively aroused (recall discussion of the Retaliatory Cycle in chapter 18). When we feel defensive, we naturally resist the threat. Resistance can take many forms. Resistance to cross-cultural training can take forms such as:

- Refusing to allow insight into one's own behavior and motivations to occur
- Doubting the validity of the information presented
- Criticizing the quality of the training program
- Perceiving the seminar leader, especially one of a minority culture, as being self-serving or prejudiced against the dominant culture
- Simply forgetting or not using the information provided.

In any case, resistance undermines awareness-building efforts to bridge culture-based differences in the organization. To be sure, cultural awareness training can be a powerful and enlightening experience for those who wish to learn. It may not be so for those on whom it is thrust.

2) Inherent bias

By conducting training primarily for the "benefit" of dominant-culture employees, providers of cultural diversity programs place the onus of responsibility on members of the dominant culture to accommodate to the needs of other groups. The program design may imply that minority-culture members already know plenty about the dominant culture's norms and values. Or, seminar designers may feel that members of minority groups do not have as much responsibility for bridging cultural differences because they are the low-power or victimized party in the cross-cultural relationship.

This bias may or may not be intended. Even when intended, it may not be explicitly stated by the seminar leader, hoping instead to bring change in a Trojan horse. But if dominant-culture employees are discriminately selected for training, or if training is directed at the "culture blindness" of the dominant-culture group, it is a message heard clearly by trainees.

Further, organizations that focus cross-cultural training on the awareness deficiencies of dominant-culture employees do a disservice to their minority and female employees: Dominance of the dominant-culture is perpetuated. How? By being given primary responsibility for change, members of the dominant-culture remain in the driver's seat – they are still in power, they are still the ones with options. Minorities are kept dependent on the choices of dominant-culture members – if a white male trainee chooses to do nothing different after attending the training program, then discrimination continues. So, awareness-based training may actually backfire. It may maintain the very power imbalance that it seeks to alter.

3) No tools

In spite of these factors, let's grant that information about cultural differences is presented, and that it is learned. Awareness is achieved. Then what? What is the program participant expected to *do* with it? What practical behavioral tools are provided that will enable him to manage those differences with minority colleagues more effectively? Too often, trainees are left in the dilemma of the automobile

mechanic who knows how to fix the problem, but lacks the tools
to apply her knowledge.

An alternative

So, what alternatives exist to training that is based only
on building cultural awareness? How can we achieve a more
integrated multicultural workforce in which differences arising
from cultural values and behavioral norms are not only
recognized, but are also effectively managed?

While disseminating information about cultural values
and norms is a well-intentioned effort, real organizational change
requires that training include behavioral *tools* – tools with which
both majority- and minority-culture employees can initiate
problem-solving dialogue. Tools that are equally powerful, no
matter whose hands are at the controls. Tools that make no
value judgment, explicitly or implicitly, about whose side of a
difference is more right. Tools that work.

Self Mediation is such a tool – indeed, it may be
regarded as a core competency of a multicultural workforce. It
empowers individuals of any ethnicity, race, sexual orientation,
and of either gender, to initiate dialogue in search of common
ground with Others. Our cultural backgrounds are one source of
differences, an important one. But differences that impair
workplace productivity arise from many sources. As individuals,
we are more than just our cultural identity. Self Mediation is a
tool for managing differences regardless of their origin – cross-
cultural or "cross-personal."

Whether you are of African, Asian, European, Hispanic,
Native American, mixed, or any other ethnic origin, and whether
you are female or male, you can empower yourself to implement
your own individual "cultural diversity program" Use Self

Mediation to engage colleagues with whom you clash in dialogue to seek mutually acceptable solutions to workplace problems. If you perceive your Other's behavior as arising from culture-based stereotypes or prejudices, those perceptions can be part of your dialogue.

Your differences on disputed workplace issues may reside in culture-based values and styles of behavior, and it is certainly worthwhile to learn how your Other differs from you in these ways. But, beneath our culture, our ethnicity, our sexual orientation, and our gender, we share fundamentally human qualities. Self Mediation draws on our basic human nature to bring us to common ground. The "forces toward harmony" discussed in chapter 19 are unique to no culture – indeed, they are not even unique to humans. Their origins lie deep in our evolutionary past, in the adaptations of the ancestors common to humans and other present-day species who display the inhibitory reflex and other behavioral responses during conflict

Culture-compatibility

To be sure, certain components of the four-step Self Mediation method are more compatible with the norms of some cultures than with others – that is, they are less unfamiliar, and so less uncomfortable, for some people than for others. But choosing to avoid the Wrong Reflexes, and taking initiative to solve an interpersonal problem, are unfamiliar and challenging tasks for most of us, no matter which culture we call home. Our tendencies to Distance and Coerce, and the Illusions from which these reflexive behaviors spring, are rooted in universal human nature. So, our reluctance to use Self Mediation is more human than it is cultural.

In fact, this practical communication tool presents an opportunity for members of non-dominant groups who find themselves disempowered by the prevailing politics of their organizations to take charge of managing differences in relationships that matter. Large-scale social change and eradication of cultural prejudice may come some day, but why wait for Godot? Act now to improve the relationships that affect you today.

Still, we have more to learn about the impact of norms and values that are endemic to particular cultures upon the effectiveness of Self Mediation. As our planet shrinks, your feedback gains value. Please report your experiences to the author in care of the publisher so future editions of this book can more authoritatively help readers manage cultural differences.

GLOSSARY

Aggression Behavior that is intended by its exhibitor to harm the interests of its target.

Ambivalence The coexistence of opposing or incompatible attitudes, needs or interests in the same individual, resulting in uncertainty about alternative courses of action.

Bad Person Illusion The perceptual phenomenon of erroneously attributing the cause of an interpersonal conflict to the defective personal characteristics of the Other.

Blips Conflicts of minor importance that are resolved or disappear spontaneously. (Level 1 conflicts)

Both-gain An attitudinal and behavioral stance by a person in conflict in which the possibility of mutually beneficial outcomes is assumed.

Boulder-in-the-Road Illusion   The phenomenon of erroneously perceiving impossibility of resolving a conflict.

Breakthrough   The occurrence during face-to-face issue-focused dialogue of a mutual shift of attitude by both partners from "me-against-you" to "us-against-the-problem."

Cardinal Rules   Guidelines for engaging in communication with others that prevent behaviors that manifest the "wrong reflexes."

Clashes   Conflicts that, if disregarded, impair the capacity of relationships to satisfy the needs of its partners. (Level 2 conflicts)

Coercion   The behavioral strategy for coping with interpersonal conflict involving the exercise or threat of force to overwhelm the resistance put forth by the Other to impose a one-sided solution (Wrong Reflex #2). See also Power-plays.

Cognitive Dissonance   The inherent discomfort resulting from experiencing two or more mental events (beliefs, attitudes, values, perceptions) that are incompatible with each other.

Conciliatory Gestures   Uncoerced behaviors, typically verbal, that display vulnerability to one's opponent in conflict.

Conflict   A condition between two interdependent people in which one or both feel angry at the other and perceive the other as being at fault.

Crises   Conflicts that threaten the continuation of a relationship. (Level 3 conflicts)

Deal   The balanced, behaviorally specific, written agreement that is reached as a result of using Self Mediation.

Dialogue The face-to-face, issue-focused verbal communication that occurs during step 3 of Self Mediation.

Difference A state of disparity in needs, values, attitudes, goals, or self-interests between two individuals in ongoing, interdependent relationship.

Distancing The behavioral strategy for coping with interpersonal conflict involving withdrawal from contact with one's adversary (Wrong Reflex #1). See also Walk-aways.

Self Mediation A behaviorally specific procedure for managing differences between people in ongoing, interdependent, two-person relationships. (Labeled "4-Step Method" in the first edition.)

Emotional Issues Matters of concern to persons in conflict that represent the psychological needs whose satisfaction is sought in the relationship.

Essential Process Face-to-face talking between two people about the issues on which they differ without interruption for as long as necessary to reach the Breakthrough.

Inhibitory Reflex The instinctive response to a conciliatory gesture displayed by an opponent in conflict, resulting in termination or suspension of aggressive behavior.

Interpersonal Pertaining to two individuals.

Issues Matters of concern to persons in conflict on which incompatible positions are held. (See Emotional, Pseudo-substantive, Substantive).

Mediation   The role of a neutral third party in facilitating the search for mutually acceptable, self-determined agreements between disputants.

Negotiation   The process of searching for agreement between people who have apparently different self-interests.

Other   One's partner in an on-going, interdependent, two-person relationship.

Polarization   The tendency toward defining opposite positions on issues in conflict.

Position   The preferred solution to a disputed issue that is put forth by a party in conflict.

Power-plays   The behaviors that implement the strategy of Coercion (Wrong Reflex #2).

Projection   The process of attributing to the Other one's unwanted feelings, attitudes, values, and beliefs that are incompatible with other such aspects of self, thereby resolving one's intrapsychic ambivalence about a disputed issue.

Pseudo-substantive Issues   Matters of concern to persons in conflict that are unconsciously represented falsely as substantive issues, but are in fact wholly or partially manifestations of emotional issues.

Retaliatory Cycle   An iterative process in which two persons in conflict engage in mutual retribution and defensive counter-attack.

Substantive Issues   Matters of concern that accurately represent the objective self-interest of the person.

Walk-aways   The behaviors that implement the strategy of Distancing (Wrong Reflex #1).

Win-Lose Illusion   The phenomenon of erroneously or prematurely assuming that no both-gain outcome is possible.

Wrong Reflexes   Automatic attitudinal and behavioral responses to conflict that derive from the "fight" and "flight" impulses. (See Distancing and Coercion).

INDEX

ACKNOWLEDGEMENTS

For their conceptual and editorial suggestions at various stages in the preparation of the first edition of this book, I am indebted to Bob Abramms, Patricia Barone, Ellen Dolsen, Susan Douglas, Linda Pleau Duffy, Barbara Durham, Tom Fiutak, Paula Flynn, Virginia Foley, Ron Heilmann, Roger Herrick, Connie Holmes, Diane Johns, Jean Johnson, Vivian Kotler, Ellie Linden, Gay Lustig, Ruthanne Marchetti, John Ogilvie, Darrel Ray, Mindy Rosenberg, Bob Schachat, Mike Schulde, Mary Ann Schwartz, George Scurlock, Elaine Stuart, Carolyn Tertes, Wallace Wilkins, and Jim Wolf.

People who have made similar contributions to the second edition include Diana Aubuchon, Nancy Boynton, Jean Dexter, Richard Keith, Phyllis Kessler, Lee Klose, Marya Muñoz, Bruce Newman, Glennis Precht, and Deborah Youngdahl.

Special thanks to Ray Rusin for planting subliminal seeds years ago that have sprouted in chapter 21, pointing the way toward future development of this work.

Greatest appreciation is reserved for Susan, Sean, and Seamus Connor – my best reasons for living long – and to best friend Susan Dana – my partner in perfecting the non-adversarial marriage.

For more information about mediation, visit

w w w . m e d i a t i o n w o r k s . c o m

ABOUT THE AUTHOR

A pioneer in the field of conflict resolution, Dan Dana is internationally recognized as the originator of Managerial Mediation. Holding the Ph.D. in psychology, Dr. Dana has served on the faculty of three universities in New England, and has been guest lecturer at institutions in Australia, New Zealand, Holland, Sweden, England, Turkey, Hong Kong, South Africa, and the former Soviet Union.

In 1985 he founded the Mediation Training Institute International as a vehicle to bring mediation to the people by means of the *Manager-as-Mediator Seminar* and the *Self-as-Mediator Seminar.*

In this book, Dan puts the tools of the professional mediator into the hands of every reader.